Fierce Imaginings

Fierce Imaginings:
The Great War, Ritual, Memory & God

Rachel Mann

DARTON·LONGMAN+TODD

First published in Great Britain in 2017 by
Darton, Longman and Todd Ltd
1 Spencer Court
140–142 Wandsworth High Street
London SW18 4JJ

ISBN 978-0-232-53278-4

A catalogue record for this book is available from the British Library

Thanks are due to the following for permission to quote copyright material:
Faber and Faber Ltd for material taken from *The Complete Poems* by Philip
Larkin; from *Personae* by Ezra Pound; from *The Waste Land* by T. S. Eliot and
from *In Parenthesis* by David Jones. Liveright Publishing Corporation for 'the
bigness of cannon'; Copyright 1923, 1951, © 1991 by the Trustees for the
E. E. Cummings Trust; Copyright © 1976 by George J. Firmage, from *Complete
Poems: 1904 – 1962* by E. E. Cummings, edited by George J. Firmage. Used by
permission of Liveright Publishing Corporation. New Directions Publishing
Corps for excerpt from 'Hugh Selwyn Mauberley' by Ezra Pound, from
Personae, copyright © 1926 by Ezra Pound. Reprinted by permission of
New Directions Publishing Corp. Jeremy Hill on behalf of the Hill Estate for
material taken from *King Log* by Geoffrey Hill.

Typeset by Kerrypress, Markyate, St Albans
Printed and bound in Great Britain by Bell & Bain, Glasgow

For the ones who never came back,
and for the ones who came back, but were never the
same.

They will call our names forever,
they will etch them all in stone;
we all have done our duty
to our families back at home;
and we will always be remembered
in the countries that we've roamed.
And at least we won't grow old.

(From *The Tree of War – A New Musical*,
written by Oliver Mills and Rachel Mann)

Contents

FOREWORD

Since 2014, we have had quite a few opportunities to think about what happened a century ago in the Great War: what was wounded, what was lost in our culture. Rachel Mann pushes our reflection on this to a new depth and a new level of challenge. Weaving together her family and local history with a sensitive reading of various signals in the wider culture, she sets out the stark truth about the loss that the First World War brought about. It was – at the most visible level – the loss of countless young people, mostly men, whose voices had never counted in the first place, in their stratified and slow-moving society; even for those who survived, it meant so often the loss of the capacity to talk about it. It was the loss of certain myths about manhood, about the possibility of victoriously negotiating pain or temporary defeat in order to manifest once again the innate strength and social durability of masculine roles. It was the loss of a God: the God who providentially ordered human history and protected his own. The real cost of violence left so many men lastingly damaged and vulnerable (Rachel Mann has some unexpected thoughts on that fictional sufferer from shell-shock, Lord Peter Wimsey); it also left the God of conventional devotion looking absurd – as that tormented prophet, 'Woodbine Willie', understood so graphically. All this is explored here with such insight and nuance.

But there is the sheer fact of the loss of all those lives – and the lasting wounds carried by men like Rachel's grandfathers, lovingly and unsentimentally evoked here. And this leads into one of the most strikingly fresh perceptions of this exceptional book. Our annual acts of remembrance are important because they give space for the affirmation of 'ordinary' lives from a century ago, give dignity to those who had so little of it acknowledged in their own lifetimes. We (liberal and pacific) modern believers find it all very complicated, and that complication is fully recognised in these pages; but we should not let the tangle of anxieties and emotions stop us grasping the colossal significance of naming and honouring the dead, the largely voiceless and powerless dead. Remembering them, not as stereotyped victims but as people with agency, emotion, sceptical humour and passionate mutual trust – this is not an empty convention but an act of faith in the fullest sense. And Rachel, with all proper reticence and all proper stubbornness, insists that we make the connection with the acts of remembering that are performed by Christians to say who they are. If we know a bit better what we're doing when we remember the slaughtered millions of the Great War, if we know that we're for once listening to the silenced and ignored voices of our fellow human beings, we can hear more profoundly the Word that speaks in the Eucharist from the pit of betrayal and 'failure'.

This is the most searching and original book I have read about the impact of the First World War on the faith and the myths of this country. Recent events have reinforced the sense that we run back to our mythology pretty readily when we feel anxious and at sea, desperately dusting off the stereotypes and the legends that seem to offer reassurance (and convenient enemies or scapegoats). The importance of this exceptional book is that it helps us see how the rituals of memory can work in a way that is anything but reactionary or repressive. They take us 'in search of the human', to use an evocative phrase from these pages: a search with some contemporary urgency.

Rowan Williams

Introduction

'What fierce imaginings their dark souls lit?'

This is a book about ghosts. Not, I hasten to add, the kind of ghouls who fill the pages of M.R. James or are conjured by the febrile minds of Hollywood screenwriters. The ghosts in these pages are both less tangible and in some respects more potent and more frightening. I am interested in the way in which certain spectres raised by and because of the Great War continue to exercise an influence and power over us. Even one hundred years on, there are any number of ways in which that particular war casts shadows over the present. The Second World War may still be 'The War' for many, and it was certainly more destructive on a global scale, yet the Great War was fundamental in shaping the character and hopes of modern Britain.

Who is this 'us' to whom I refer? Well, in the first instance I'm honest enough to admit I'm talking about 'me'. I am and always have been fascinated by the events which scarred and effectively remade the European, and specifically, the English 'Mind' between 1914 and 1918. I have read countless books about both the Great War and its cultural impact. Indeed, the fact that I'm inclined to refer to it as 'The Great War' rather than World War One is revealing. Is it because, at some level, I'm caught up in the elegiac romanticism that the former designation evokes? Does the very term 'Great' indicate that I am, in some sense, dazzled by this war? Well, I'm certainly fascinated by it and my attention is drawn to the claim that the Great War represents, mythologically, the death of innocence and, more than that, the death of a certain confident self-understanding of what it means to be English or British.[1] It sets out for many the very texture of loss. And, yes, if I'm honest, there is something within me that mourns (either pathetically or bathetically) the loss of the myth of unabridged hope, the myth of an unquestioned Englishness.[2] At the same time, I see the myths for what they are – something that if they were ever foundational were hardly life-giving (except for a privileged minority) and are not life-giving now. I am glad that bogus notions of what it means to be British should be challenged at every turn. And yet, I know I carry within me a set of myths, laid and overlaid by a particular kind of rural white working-class upbringing, which dance around the totem pole of remembrance, memory and war. Myths that, thirty plus years ago, were still etched into the sad, heavy faces of my grandfathers. Myths symbolised by a thousand cenotaphs and countless crosses of remembrance.

The 'us' of which I speak, then, is not simply an excuse to talk about me. Both my grandfathers, and, therefore, ultimately my grandmothers, my parents and my whole family have been caught up in the effects and the after-effects of the Great War. This book, then, is about memory and the way war is memorialised. Partly, this will entail examining my family memory and my own attempt to comprehend the memories I have of my grandparents and place them in a family story. But if it is a personal exploration, there is a profound sense in which – for a large section of the British population – my grandfathers' stories and my family's story are everyone's story.

We all carry the war within us, or rather, we all carry certain stories about the war within us. These include standardised 'myths' like the notion of 'The Lions Led By Donkeys'. The poetry of Wilfred Owen has ensured that we imagine the war in particular ways. The iconic photographic images of the war – vast wastelands of mud and broken trees – populate our inner landscapes. But more than that, it is worth restating the obvious: the Great War was a cultural and social catastrophe. Three quarters of a million British men and women were killed in four years and countless others maimed, wounded and emotionally destroyed. Another quarter of a million men from the Dominions and Colonies died defending the Empire of which they were either willingly or unwillingly part.[3] The focal point of this destruction was a relatively small section of Flanders and Picardy that was characterised by long periods of military stasis. Britain had not seriously been at war for a hundred years and in that time had become the most extraordinarily extended and potent empire in history. In six years of the Second World War, Britain lost less than half that number of lives. Part of this is surely down to improved medicine – not least to the discovery of penicillin – as well as the fact that the decisive front was in Eastern Europe. Truly the Great War was a catastrophe for the English Mind. One token of this is how long it took for memoirs of the war to emerge. Writings by figures we now connect definitively with the war – Sassoon, Graves, Blunden and Brittain – only became popular ten or so years after the war. The war generated vast cultural repression and psycho-social damage.

Furthermore, there is that other fact which echoes into almost everyone's story: the British army was a citizen army. The pre-war professional army of about 100,000 men – the army which came to be known as *The Old Contemptibles* – was effectively destroyed by early 1915. The men who volunteered for war in 1914 – searching for adventure and escape, who volunteered to be with friends and, perhaps, even for King and Country – were mostly very ordinary, non-military lads. It's standard to talk of *The Lost Generation*, often thinking romantically of the university volunteers, of the posh chaps in Ford Madox Ford's *Parade's End* or Vera Brittain's *Testament of Youth*, but most of Kitchener's Million were folk like my grandfathers – labourers, farm hands, shop workers, mill hands and clerks. An army which, as Richard Holmes evocatively puts it, 'were the best of the nation's voluntary manhood, and the merest glance at its casualty roll shows what the Somme did to the old world of brass bands and cricket fields, pit-head cottages and broad acres.'[4] And beyond them came the conscripts. For the first time in England's history there was a draft. Our grandparents and great-grandparents carried our stories off to war and we have never been the same. Lives, whose only historical marks had lain in parish registers, became inscribed in the annals of military history. Nearly a million ended up with names carved into Portland stone in foreign fields.

This, then, is also a book about how I relate to the concept of 'Britain' or, dare I say it, 'England'. I am clear in my mind that I am not a nationalist. Equally, I find the notion of patriotism troubling. Such is our imperial past and such has been my liberal education that saying I'm patriotic feels troubling. I am able to enjoy 'being' English or British in certain sporting contexts in an unalloyed way, but, in my heart, I feel there is something tasteless about unthinking pride in an accident of birth. And yet ... I am a romantic about England. It wasn't until I experienced living abroad in my early twenties that I properly began to appreciate how English I was. As I've gotten older I've been drawn to what might be called the pastoral mystery of England. For England does not seem to me to reside especially in the urban, but in the beauty of her coast or the hills of Cumbria and the gentle fields of the Shires. And if we are mostly city dwellers and urbanites – and indeed I have become one – I am still mesmerised by another England: an England of county towns and villages, of settled existence and community. An England that – even in an age of social media and instant communication – seems mostly bewildered by the urbane, cosmopolitan world people like me inhabit. And if this picture of England is both romantic and foolish it nonetheless exercises an effect. In one sense, the rupture of the Great War sealed all that went before it in a kind of romantic aspic. It is one of the trigger points for our modern hunger for a return to a world that is more innocent and less sullied.

And, of course, this book is also an attempt to meditate on the place of God and the divine in our pictures of the Great War. One of the stories that gets told about the war was that it killed God for many of its participants, that it signalled the terminal decline of the Church of England and, indeed, of Christian faith in England. One suspects that a lot of inflated rhetoric gets spoken of here. Astute church historians like Alan Wilkinson suggest that the Church of England was not only in a kind of crisis before the War, but perhaps is always in a state of crisis. And yet there are some important theological and cultural insights to be drawn out of the war. Philip Jenkins correctly claims that 'the First World War was a thoroughly religious event in the sense that overwhelmingly Christian nations fought each other in what many viewed as a holy war, a spiritual conflict.'[5] Albert Marrin persuasively argues that the war killed off a certain sort of repellent 'militarism' within the Church of England which has meant that it can never again dare act as a recruiting sergeant for state violence. But there is also something more mythic I will attempt to tease out. My instinct is that if God was not killed on the Somme and at Ypres, some conceptions of 'him' were. These battles were the death knell for some patriarchal, imperialistic conceptions of God. They revealed him – the wise old man who intuitively we wish to trust – to be an idol with clay (indeed, muddy and waterlogged) feet. And if that idol rightly fell it does not follow that we do not mourn his loss. One imagines that the Israelites mourned the destruction of their Golden Calf. We so often mourn the destruction of the golden idols we have made for our own benefit. And in the rituals of remembrance that emerged out of the war and have become folk memory in our culture, a whole new kind of civic religion emerged, tangled between the rubble of Christian faith and civic duty. We live in the fragments of loss still and we have yet to learn how to be whole.

If I am carrying myths about identity and the Great War around, like one of those vast backpacks the Tommies wore, I am trying to lay them down. And yet because they are myths – that is, truth-bearing stories which inform who we are – it is so very hard. When the Armistice was finally called, the soldiers carried forward the war into their lives, unable to lay down the memories. Indeed, there is a profound sense in which, as Geoff Dyer has suggested, the war has remembrance inscribed into its very nature. We carry those memories still and we are dazzled both by the world it tore up, imagined as a place of innocence, and the world come of age it left behind. Or if it is not a matter of laying down a set of myths, then I am trying to come to terms with my cultural inheritance and my family's part in it. I am most definitely not the first to explore the curious intersection of familial, cultural, military and national symbols generated by the war. In many ways this book is a footnote to others, especially the work of Geoff Dyer, Modris Eksteins and Paul Fussell. I hope its freshness lies in the sensitivity and nuance a philosophically and theologically-alert writer can bring to myth and symbol. They are, after all, the religious person's everyday reality. Indeed, one of the problems our secular society faces is an inability to acknowledge how much all of us, religious or not, live by myth and symbol.

This book takes its title from a line in Isaac Rosenberg's poem, 'Dead Man's Dump'. The poem captures a scene behind the front line where the dead pile up, waiting for burial. The poem is both brutally unsentimental – Rosenberg describes how the wheels of the gun carriage 'lurched over sprawled dead/But pained them not' – and yet mythic. He comments on how 'Earth has waited for them/All the time of their growth/Fretting for their decay.' Insofar as this book is a tribute to the missing of Passchendaele and the Somme, among whom I count my grandfathers, I hope it avoids childish sentimentality. However, I also hope it speaks into the mythic horizons of the Great War. My grandfathers both survived, though they were never quite the same again. Loss became inscribed in their lives and the lives of their families. While I cannot hope to reconstruct my grandfathers' lost voices, this book aims faithfully to examine the 'fierce imaginings their dark souls lit'. In doing so, I hope this book is spacious. That is, that it doesn't simply use my grandparents or other members of my family for my own ends. I also hope that my aim to be honest about cultural 'totems' and symbols like Country, Faith and Family does not leave me over-exposed. I want to steer a difficult path – between the 'holy' conviction of those who claim war is always wrong and the fearsome passion of those whose hackles rise at any questions raised about Britain's prosecution of international affairs. I hope that, at the end of this book, I get to walk away with some measure of dignity left intact. For, if this is an act of laying out and laying down, I want to do this in such a way that the inheritance, the stories and the discourses into which the myths feed are places of energy and life.

Explanatory note on reading this book
Because it centres on the 1914–18 War, some readers of this book might expect it to count primarily as 'history'. My invitation, however, is to read this book as an extended meditation on 'identity' and the symbols and rituals we use to shape it. Each chapter uses a symbol, object or idea – 'the Flanders' Poppy', 'A battlefield' – as a point of departure. It does so in order to interrogate not only the meaning of war and remembrance, but their place in our cultural and psychological identities. As in prayer and meditation, ideas and themes overlap and interweave, not so much to generate a linear argument, but to invite new reflections on ourselves, our communities and the world.

Particular thanks are due to Susie Snyder, Daisy Black, Andrew Mann, Albert Radcliffe, Jeffrey Wainwright and Angelica Michelis for carefully reading early drafts and improving this book incalculably.

Prologue

My mum and I are driving into Worcester. It is the week after Christmas and it's one of those grey low-ceiling days on which crows seem to caw-caw for the end of the world. We are on the old 449 road driving past 1930s semis and shops for paint and bric-a-brac and we have settled into an amicable silence. And then on the right I see a park, a tiny park of grass and stripped ash, announcing itself from a brick entrance with sculpted wreaths as 'Gheluvelt Park' and I am cast back into one of those endless puzzles of my childhood. For in spotting the name I am, momentarily, my eight-year-old self again clicked safely into the back of my parents' Vauxhall Chevette on our way to visit my dad's aunts. And I'm puzzling out how to say this peculiar word 'Gheluvelt' (Helluvell, Gelluvult, Gulluvelt) and what on earth it has to do with Worcester.

Yet even at eight I connect the word with my grandfathers, one of whom, Sam, has already been dead for four years. Grandad Sam – who brought us packets of sweets and carried great bags of sadness under his eyes. Grandad Sam, my dad's dad, the twinkling man who years later I discover had beaten the shit out of my granny when he got pissed or just couldn't hide the memories of the war, the Great War, the war that took him outside his beloved country for the only time in his life. So, now, Mum and I are passing Gheluvelt Park again and I remember that my intuitive connection of it at eight with my grandfathers was not so very far out. For, both Grandad Sam and Bert were soldiers of the Great War and, as I discovered in my teens, Gheluvelt Park was one of those small grassy memorial spaces that were carved out of its silence. (Gheluvelt being one of those now forgotten butchering places of the Ypres Salient where, in 1914, the Worcestershire Regiment fought.)

The Great War represents a crisis in my family history. By this, I mean that it represents the point at which my family took part in History for the first time. Before the war my family's only mark on public space lay in the pages of parish registers when they were 'hatched, matched and despatched' along with the rest of the rural poor. When the war began my grandfathers were swept up into another life. They received army numbers, joined regiments, got wounded and, ultimately, received medals.[1] What had been generations of agricultural existence were for the first time questioned, if not yet broken. Questioned, but not broken for, as both Bert and Sam discovered, life in the army was the continuation of agricultural labour by other means; they had as Ronald Blythe puts it, 'fled the wretchedness of the land in 1914'[2] only to discover an intensification of it in Flanders and Picardy. For, if it wasn't handling horses it was digging. They were yeomen made the makers of what Paul Fussell calls the Troglodyte World, burying bodies and the remains of bodies, digging deeper so as to make safer places or better places for killing. Digging and redigging the same damn piece of waterlogged land night after night. It's hard not to believe, despite the grimness of life on the land in 1914, that as Sam and Bert crouched in trenches they didn't sometimes think longingly of the days before the war. A time when a long day in the fields at least offered the promise of cider and sleep for weary bones rather than the threat of death.[3] Grandad Sam was also a horseman. Indeed, one strand of the family – being short of stature and lightweight – successfully went in for jockeying on the race tracks of France and England. And this understanding of horses got Sam out of the trenches into another life – as trooper in the Worcestershire Yeomanry in Allenby's desert campaign and batman to the 4th Baron Hampton.

Grandad Bert (my mum's dad) was a private in the Worcestershire regiment and, later, after being seriously wounded, in the Labour Corps.[4] I only knew him as an exceptionally quiet old man who loved Saturday afternoon wrestling – Giant Haystacks versus Big Daddy versus Catweazle versus Kendo Nagasaki – and watching snooker on black and white TV. His natural habitat always seemed to be outdoors and his whole life – apart from some time working at the local RAF base – was orientated around the land, primarily as a farm labourer. If he had ever been a dreamer or a man of words I do not know. It only seemed to me that his past had silenced him.

Ronald Blythe is right. In 1914, agricultural conditions were harsh. They were perhaps closer to the bleak narratives of Hardy than the pastoral idylls conjured by Vaughan Williams at his most expressive. If George Butterworth's *A Shropshire Lad* song cycle beautifully evokes the shires and a world about to disappear in the carnage of war,[5] it is a romantic evocation. Granny Collins told a story that reminds us not to be sentimental about the Victorian and Edwardian eras. As a little girl, before the war, one of her jobs in her Worcestershire village was to ring the bell for funerals. She'd often be dragged out of school to do it. One day, as she tolled the bell, she saw her father enter the church carrying a tiny coffin. Puzzled, she realised it was her infant sister. It was the first she knew about her death.

In the days before mechanisation of the Land and in conditions of low wages, the army would certainly have provided promises of escape for someone like young Albert and his brother Tom (who was killed on the Mesopotamian Front). For over a hundred years before the Great War, the countryside had been haemorrhaging people. From 1881, 700,000 British agricultural workers and their families, helped by the new National Union of Agricultural Workers, emigrated to the colonies. Two and half million acres of arable land became grass between 1872 and 1900 and the invention of devices like the binder meant that fewer labourers were needed. Equally, the promise of the city and the town, the dream of weaving riches and a better life in the looms of Kidderminster or Manchester or Oldham had emptied the land. The situation presented to those who remained was no romantic idyll. Steven Spielberg's glossy picture of 1914 rural Devon in the early sections of his film adaptation of *War Horse* is hardly faithful to reality. Long hours of work with few comforts and little security and even less entertainment were the norm. If life at the Manor House was good, life in the Cottage held few delights and typically offered only wearied bones.

I have met people who have within them a seemingly inexhaustible stillness. Among them I count assorted holy people, those who have accepted they are about to die and others who are not enamoured with the glamour of this world. I have also known people who have an extraordinary facility with silence, an aspect of character I find both rarer and more impressive as our world becomes noisier. Grandad Bert was not a man for stillness. He was at ease with a hoe in his hand, working out the rural choreography of centuries in the easy movements of his body and tools. And yet, from the point of view of a small child, it was as if his short, plump frame and his loose jowls gathered silence to itself. Even when his wife, Doll, aka Granny Collins, was still alive, it seemed to me that he had nothing to say. Granny had all the words, was full of stories and rumours and gossip. His silence said more than all of her remarkable words. But if I remember granny's love and silly stories, and the way she would paint kitchen cupboards bright orange, it is Bert who haunts me now. Perhaps because I remember him speaking only once.

As a small child I became fascinated by war, read endless tales about derring-do. I loved magazines like *The Victor* and made models of WW1 and WW2 aeroplanes. I knew grandad had fought in the Great War and yet I knew it was something we did not, as a family, talk about. Or if we did, we did not do so in his company. Yet I remember once asking him about his experience in the war. He didn't raise his voice. He didn't seem angry. He spoke quietly about being wounded on the Somme. I was excited. I'd heard of this place. I'd read about it in magazines and books. It made me think of heroes and courage and glory. I asked where else he'd fought, with the childish and insensitive passion of the child who only thinks of glory and doesn't yet appreciate the pain. He mumbled some places I'd not heard of, finally mentioning another familiar place, Passchendaele. I asked him what it was like to have been a soldier. He looked at me sadly and with a finality I could not challenge, and said, simply, 'Passchendaele was the worst.'

It is perhaps impossible for a child to properly appreciate that their parents, let alone their grandparents, were ever young. Even now, as a middle-aged woman, when I look at the photos of Sam and Bert as old men and compare them with the rare images of them as young men I still can't quite believe it. As I reconsider that memory of Bert talking in such an understated, taciturn manner about being at Passchendaele, the place that has become the icon of that war's beastliness, I find it harder still. For any creature – man or beast – to have lived through that is surely impossible. On 18 July 1917, the British and Canadian forces began laying down a barrage that, come the initial assault on 31 July, had expended four and a quarter million shells. That autumn of 1917, the naturally high water-table of Flanders was tipped into disaster by constant bombardment and unseasonal levels of rain. It was the season of the war when if the shells and the bullets didn't get you, the bottomless shell holes would. To step off the duckboards could spell death. Man and beast would simply be sucked under.

There is that famous photo of Canadian machine gunners in the wasteland of the battlefield. At first you can barely distinguish them from the landscape. It is as if it is absorbing them, their sodden, muddy uniforms becoming simply another feature of the broken ground. The gunners have no real identity anymore. They have become the war and the war them. Which is another way of registering the thought, 'How could any human being have been in that place and remained a human being?' And somehow

I find it even more bewildering to think of a young man, even with military training, cast into that. Bert would have been barely twenty-one years old when he experienced Passchendaele. And, yes, the young are resilient and capable of the most extraordinary things perhaps precisely because they are discovering the world for the first time. The world had grown very old by the autumn of 1917 and the likes of Bert had long since lost their innocence. He was no virgin to violence. The older I get, however, the less I can comprehend how any of those young men did not completely collapse. It is true that there were quiet sectors in the Great War:[6] it is also true that men were fed in and out of the line reasonably frequently, but all writers seem to agree that the Ypres Salient – which Passchendaele was supposed to break (and barely shifted from late 1914 till 1918) – was constantly 'hot'. And in October 1917 it became, as a result of unseasonal weather, the iconic quagmire of our most terrible imaginings.

I think of my nephews – young men, or soon to become young men – and know they might choose a military career. They might be trained in the instruments of violence and be sent to 'foreign fields'. But they are children to me. When we are young we think we are so grown up, but I look at Mike and Alex or Sam and Tom and they seem barely formed. I cannot imagine throwing Mike, good strong lad that he is, into the vile fields of Flanders. And yet he is practically the same age as Bert was when he saw too much. To develop the character to live life well is a lifetime's work and youths like Bert saw more than those of us who have grown old or middle-aged in the privileged 'West' have ever seen. Somewhere in the midst of that truth lies a mystery. For surely any sane person would be desperate to spare not only their loved ones, but anyone the knowledge of war's vileness. Yet the fact that men like Bert came home and found some way, any way, to take up the threads of a lost life is deeply moving. Indeed, more than that, part of our call to remember them lies in the truth that they faced the impossible and, whether they were killed or physically maimed or emotionally shattered, they found some way to carry on. In most cases, they made a home, raised children, and found some way to act for the good.

In the piles of photographs of family weddings and Christenings and holidays, among that family catalogue of bad hairdos, uncomfortable uncles, and (to borrow a phrase of Larkin's) 'rapidly re-adjusted ties' is a spotted blotched photo of a group of uniformed men driving a piece of artillery across a sepia wasteland. My dad tells me this is a picture of his dad, yet he doesn't know which of the figures in the landscape he is. Grandad could be the one on the second right. He could be any one of these men. Geoff Dyer, in his classic study of the Great War and visual culture, draws out how the war supplied a series of myths which every family and soldier got caught up in. So, for example, my dad tells the story about how grandad had this pocket watch, which he'd lent to his best mate John Godwin in the trenches. The pocket watch, I was told, saved John Godwin's life, a bullet just bounced off. As a child I lapped it up. Only later did I realise that all families had this story, either a pocket watch or Bible saving someone's life. It was everyone's story. My grandad could be any of the men in the photo. He could be any soldier. He could be anyone's grandad.[7]

CHAPTER ONE

'Cenotaph' – How public monuments make it easier to forget

With few exceptions, if we are remembered at all it is as names. Indeed, often those names come down to 'pet' names – mum, dad, granny, grandpa, aunty and uncle. Sometimes, and perhaps increasingly, these names are attached to photos and digital images. It is the fate of few to be remembered for long. Our great cities are littered with statues and memorials to those who, for all intents and purposes, have already been forgotten. For even if some names still shine bright in civic records how many really care for the identities of the great and the good who stand solemnly over us on faux-Roman plinths? For the most part, when we go to the public square in Manchester or Liverpool or London and gaze up at the heroes of the past we see nothing in the marble. Indeed, in Delhi, there is that famous 'backlot' of imperial statues and mementoes that were torn down by an administration freeing itself from England's imperial adventuring. The fate of Shelley's *Ozymandias* – the fate of all imperial adventurers and regimes that imagine they shall last a thousand years – is the fate of us all.

The Cenotaph on Whitehall is a replacement for a temporary structure erected for the Victory parade in 1919. To paraphrase Geoff Dyer, the Great War was, in a profound sense, not fought to be won, but to be remembered. And, thus, the public demanded that the temporary structure created for victory became a permanent memorial to all who had died. Its very nature – as an empty tomb, rather than a catafalque such as that erected for the French victory parade – was to hold all who had been lost. Indeed, the nature of its design, using the architectural trick known as *entasis*, underlines this. For the sides of Sir Edwin Landseer Lutyens' work are not parallel. They curve in such a way that if you were to trace them to the top and bottom a kind of sphere would form, the points only meeting nine hundred feet above and below ground. A vast space still much too small to encompass the lost.

I remember my first pilgrimage to it as a fourteen year old; how, on my first ever visit to London, as part of a school trip, I sought it out, or (perhaps) it sought me out. While others marvelled with provincial eyes at the crowds on Oxford Street, ten deep, or delighted at the sheer excess of Harrods, I was thrilled when a few of us got to head to Whitehall. Some were keen to see the Houses of Parliament from across Westminster Bridge. I had eyes only for the absent dead. If only I could find them. Because that was the shock. I knew from watching the Remembrance Sunday parades what the Cenotaph looked like; that it was a sacral space carved out of the pain of the nation, set aside for solemnity, for old men and women reliving old dreams, nightmares and past glories. And I could not see it, despite it rising over ten metres above street level, because of the noise and traffic.

In my naivety I had not imagined that the silence of that empty tomb would be allowed to be overwhelmed by the banal, the scream and thump of the everyday.

It seemed to me then that allowing the everyday to encroach on the Cenotaph was an act of sacrilege. For watching the Remembrance Sunday parade had long been part of my personal ritual. As a small child I would sit in front of the television, a huge brown box, made with plastic that was supposed to look like wood. The screen exuded the kind of static electricity that grabs your hair when you get close to it. And I sat in front of it watching the bleak peculiar stillness and movement of 'Remembrance Sunday' live from the Cenotaph. My mum wanted me to go to church, but I would not. Not even the opportunity to laugh at my brother in his comedy Cub Scout uniform processing to and from church would drag me away. I was transfixed.

Every year till I was well into my twenties and I'd become a Christian and found other things to do on a Sunday, I was mesmerised and would not move. Even now, as a priest, before I head out to lead worship on Remembrance Sunday, I will turn the telly on, wanting to stay and watch, as if preparing for what I must do elsewhere. Remembrance Sunday was the day each year on which I, a wild excitable child, stopped, settled by the fire and simply goggled. Goggled at the stiff choreography of figures so ancient they were surely made of stone and animated by a magical spell. Absorbed by the solemn, formal music. I could not understand why no one else from my family watched with me. I could not understand how my dad could be outside tinkering with a motorbike, or my mum preparing lunch, for surely this event was a tremendous thing.[1] To use language I've learnt since, it was to me at nine, a ritual speaking into transcendence and vice versa. And here I was, a strange child, finding communion in a cold November ritual. Alone of my family, Grandad Bert watched – and he watched alone. Mum told me years later that this was because he hated anyone seeing him cry.

My first experience of leading worship on Remembrance Sunday came as an ordinand. I waited in the vestry of a country church, about to step out to lead the people in their prayers of remembrance. I felt uncomfortable and inadequate (and not simply because I hadn't done one of these services before). I knew there were veterans (of World War Two and Korea) present, men and women who had been party to terrible things. I asked myself, 'What have I, a green young woman, got to say to them?' Indeed, what the hell were we remembering anyway? I knew that I was going to talk about sacrifice and duty in my sermon, but I was uncomfortable about talking about them in this context – their religious and martial connotations have been too readily associated together in the past. It was not until we said the following words that I began to feel I was on shared, confident ground:

> *They shall grow not old, as we that are left grow old:*
> *Age shall not weary them, nor the years condemn.*
> *At the going down of the sun and in the morning*
> *We will remember them.*

Every year on Remembrance Sunday these words of Laurence Binyon's are intoned.[2] Geoff Dyer suggests, 'We know them – more or less – by heart. They seem not to have been written, but to have pulsed into life in the nation's collective memory, to have been generated, down the long passage of years, by the hypnotic spell of Remembrance they are used to induce.'[3] But as Alan Wilkinson, among others, notes the words were written in September 1914, before most of the fallen actually fell. Wilkinson calls them 'remarkably prescient':[4] Dyer makes the startling claim that Binyon's poem is a work of anticipation, 'or more accurately, the *anticipation of remembrance*, a foreseeing that is also a determining.'[5]

Indeed, even while it was being fought, the war had the character of looking forward to the time when it would be remembered. So, for example, Henri Barbusse's 1916 book *Le Feu/ Under Fire* (a direct influence on Sassoon and Owen) insists that such was the intensity of the experience of the Great War that those who lived through it will be condemned to forget it. One of the characters provides an extensive and detailed litany of all the things that will be forgotten, from 'the endless vigils' through the 'foul wounds' through to 'the counter-attacks.'[6] Of course, this litany of 'forgetfulness' serves only to guarantee one thing: that they shall be remembered, even if they shall only be remembered as 'names'. A memorial of nomenclature is constructed from that which will be forgotten.

We are inclined to think that the urge towards memorialisation lies in our desire to commemorate and recognise significant things, persons and events. This is certainly one authentic motivation. We do not wish to forget that 'this' happened 'here'. There is another less explored dimension. The urge to remember and memorialise is one reaction to our fragility and impermanence. It is our knowledge of and our fear of our fragility which drives us towards memorialisation. Perhaps the great memorials – the cenotaphs and the tombs of the Unknown Soldier found in the capitals of so many of the War's combatant nations – are acts of resistance to time and fragility and an attempt to wrestle with the enormous sin of being frivolous with so much fragility. Our memorials are attempts at a kind of 'civic atonement' for the most terrible sin.

The poet Pindar suggests that, 'Human excellence/grows like the vine tree/fed by the green dew.'[7] There is a profound sense in which our very humanity, our very wonder as creatures, lies in our fragility, impermanence and capacity for change. As I, and others, have noted, we are not called to be like the gods – hard, unchanging and sleek.[8] And herein lies one of the problems with memorialisation: the moment we attempt to 'make' people in stone and marble we betray them. Our strategies of making immortality cast the remembered into the long night of slow erosion at the hands of the elements and social fashion. In Manchester there is another Lutyens' Cenotaph. Until recently, it was placed in the midst of one of the busiest thoroughfares of the city. Thousands drove and walked past it every day. Trams stopped yards from it and commuters spilled out and saw nothing. Even now that the council has moved the monument to its own quieter, more focused space, we are caught up in our phones and busyness and the need to be elsewhere. Nobody knows or cares what a cenotaph is. The public silence is overwhelmed by commerce and trams and music piped, via iPods, directly into our ears. We forget what we should remember; we cannot see what is before our very eyes. At best we manage to notice the dead for one day a year, stilling ourselves on

Remembrance Sunday. So often, the two minutes of remembrance makes it safe to forget them for the rest of the year.

Perhaps the mistake of our forebears was to attempt to achieve the illusion of immutability. Of course, it is reasonable to ask, 'How could they not?' England, the United Kingdom, Britain, whatever you want to call it, has never experienced human disaster on the scale of the Great War. Even if the Second World War was, in terms of the UK mainland, more destructive and terrifying for the civilian population, the numbers of UK folk killed, wounded and missing simply pale in comparison with the Great War. And, of course, the Great War happened at the zenith of British imperial power and in a context where Britain had not been involved in a truly major European conflict for one hundred years. The implications of industrial warfare on human flesh in an age without adequate tactics, medicine or communications had already been demonstrated by the American Civil War and the Franco-Prussian War. However, the Edwardian English – living lives that were admittedly less settled and idyllic than myth would sometimes have us believe – were simply in no position to appreciate the shape of total war. The psycho-social wounds gouged by four years of total war was so unanticipated and so devastating that, in the post-war era, the nation simply had to find a way to remember. And it had to do so in such a way that no one would forget.

We are fragile, impermanent creatures passing briefly through time. It is the urge of many of us, especially in an individualistic setting where the cult of self is dominant, to lay down markers of our existence. Of course this is no mere late modern phenomenon. A visit to one of the great UK cemeteries like Highgate or Manchester's Southern, both created in the nineteenth century, instructs us in how strong our desire for some permanent marker is. Indeed, in one sense the urge towards the permanent personal memorial came of age in Victorian England. Whereas earlier generations, stirred by the perceived close proximity of divine judgment, settled rural life and the importance of the church, sought to be buried close by the parish church, later ones took advantage of the opportunities afforded by the civil authorities – vast, well laid out fields of memory disconnected from the judgment of church and God. Here the living were invited to contemplate mortality, but also remember the dead free from concerns of ultimate Judgment.

The abiding mood of the new municipal cemetery was 'sleep'. Here the dead could go to eternal rest. Consciously or subconsciously this move to a mood of rest or eternal sleep was indicative of the growing unease about the mechanisation of life and the destruction of the self that it can indicate. Ironically, as industry threatened the distinctiveness of human identity, the idea of 'the individual' became more important. As early as 1829, Thomas Carlyle drew attention to how new distributions of wealth, fostered by industrialisation, had begun to restructure old established relationships. 'The Mechanical Age' alienates 'the labourer' from the 'products of labour'. Carlyle claims, 'our old modes of exertion are all discredited, and thrown aside. On every hand, the living artisan is driven from his workshop, to make room for a speedier, inanimate one.'[9] 'Cultural' production – traditionally in the hands of the skilled artisan – is replaced by the machine and the mechanical process. Yet, as if to reassert the need for the great individual in the face of his own bleak assessment of the nineteenth century, Carlyle develops his famous 'Great Man' thesis. In *On Heroes, Hero-Worship & the Heroic in History*, intended as an exploration of the implications of *Sartor Resartus*, Carlyle proposes an account of history and culture in terms of 'great men'. As W.H. Hudson argues, in his introduction to *On Heroes*, 'The Great Man is supreme. He is not the creature of his age, but its creator; nor its servant, but its master. "The History of the World is but the Biography of Great Men."'[10] In the Mechanical Age, Carlyle offers the Hero as 'Prophet' and 'Poet' as an attempt to address the belatedness and secondary nature of 'Man'.

In an age where 'Man' was becoming secondary to the industrial processes 'he'd' created, the new municipal cemeteries asserted the dignity of the individual and his 'right' to 'rest'. If life, especially in the towns and cities, was gaining the character of the machine, then surely death could offer a person dignity and rest. Anxiety about the fate of the self in life was countered by the assurance of rest in death.[11] Even as the new technology of cremation was introduced and became normal, those who could afford it, sought memorialisation. The walls of Manchester's Old Chapel at the Crematorium are covered with hundreds of names – the names of the respectable, the shopkeepers, the inflowing workers from field and other lands attracted by Cottonopolis' presumed Streets of Gold. Yet so many of the names on that wall are as unknown and lost as those to whom there is no memorial.

In 1986, conceptual artists Jochen and Esther Gerz created, at the invitation of the city of Hamburg, what they called a *Gegen-Denkmal* or 'counter-monument'. This twelve metre plus pillar was supposed to be a 'Monument against Fascism, War, and Violence – and for Peace and Human Rights.' James E. Young[12] records how the artists had two concerns: first, how to create something that would enable the community to take responsibility for remembrance and action and, second, to build a monument which would not buy into what they saw as the fascistic tendencies in all monuments. 'What we did not want,' Jochen Gerz declared, 'was an enormous pedestal with something on it presuming to tell people what they ought to think.' Their solution, as Young puts it, would be 'a monument against itself: against the traditionally didactic function of monuments, against their tendency to displace the past they would have us contemplate – and finally against the authoritarian propensity in all art that reduces viewers to passive spectators.'[13]

And thus the Gerzs created a monument that disappeared. It was self-effacing and self-abnegating and had its own absence built into its presence. Hamburg offered them a pretty park space for the monument. Instead the Gerzs chose what they called a 'normal, uglyish place'. It would become one more eyesore among thousands of brutal, urban eyesores. It was located in Harburg, the part of the city populated by Turkish immigrant workers and the urban poor. The monument itself was twelve metres high and one metre square, made of hollow aluminium and plated with a layer of soft, easily graffitied lead. At the base – in German, French, Hebrew, English, Russian, Arabic and Turkish – an inscription read, 'We invite the citizens of Harburg, and visitors to the town, to add their names here to ours. In doing so, we commit ourselves to remain vigilant. As more and more names cover this twelve-metre tall lead column, it will gradually be lowered into the ground. One day it will have disappeared completely and the site of the Harburg monument against fascism will be empty. In the end, it is only we ourselves who can rise up against injustice.'

The Gerzs produced a memorial which, while generating its own kind of ritual and remembrance through the inscription of names, also ensured that if it was for 'all time' it was also predicated on its own self-effacement. This was a memorial designed to disappear, to enact the fragility of memory and rehearse a fundamental truth – memory is not something fixed, but to be constantly renewed through our commitments and activity. There is an echo here of the fundamental Christian activity of Eucharist. In the assembly of faith, priest and people gather to re-enact the breaking of bread and wine outpoured, participating in an activity of remembrance that is also communion and a renewal of commitment to service. The Christian re-membering of Christ is a constant practice of making 'present' and yet is a disappearing act. The embodiment of Christ in organic matter – in bread and wine – is a constant re-inscription of fragility. Christ is not made to be cast in bronze or gold or stone like an idol. Christ is precisely not the Golden Calf.

In 2013, the South African artist Paul Emmanuel's work *The Lost Men of France* was selected to be included in France's official commemorations for the one-hundred-year anniversary of the outbreak of war. Erected at the Thiepval Memorial on which 72,000 names of missing British and South African servicemen who fought at the Somme with no known grave are inscribed, the memorial art work comprises a 600m stretch of 'large, fragile, semi-transparent silk banners'. It included the names of black and white South African servicemen and the names of soldiers from the other Allied Forces, as well as those of German soldiers who died in battlefields all over the Western Front.

As Emmanuel himself said, it was intended to 'be a non-partisan artwork and makes no political statements'. That is moot. One of the striking facts about Lutyens' 45-metre high brick Thiepval Memorial – which dominates the old Somme battlefield for miles around – is that the names of missing black South African soldiers are themselves missing. It inscribes a profound act of forgetting or erasure. It reminds us that the Great War was an imperial war in which many not only went missing, but were systematically forgotten. As Emmanuel adds, 'The Lost Men of France' was intended as 'An anti-monument, it does not glorify war but asks questions about masculinity and vulnerability…It questions the exclusion of certain people in traditional memorials – in particular black South African servicemen.' The names were photographed after being pressed into the artist's body, without reference to rank, nationality or ethnicity. The banners were to be hung in the landscape and 'left to the wind'. When I visited the Thiepval Memorial in Spring 2016 there were no banners left.

The Cenotaph on Whitehall is, in one sense, the precise opposite of Emmanuel's monument at Thiepval or the Gerzs' monument in Hamburg. It is the essence of an imperial ideology that wishes to instruct the viewer on how the object is to be received. When we see it – on TV or directly – it is designed to communicate silence and solemnity. It holds within itself the classical pretensions of all empires. It will not be moved or gainsaid. It is our task to move or orientate ourselves around it. This 'story of itself' is only underlined by the ritual assigned to it. Each year the great and the good gather around it. The survivors and the relatives of survivors process past, acting as the surrogate dead. In those justly famous words of T.S. Eliot from 'The Waste Land': 'Under the brown fog of a winter dawn,/A crowd flowed over London Bridge, so many,/I had not thought death had undone so many'.[14] In the immediate post-war years the crowds were vast. They have, inevitably, changed over the past one hundred years, but still the people come to bear witness in the heart of official Britain, responding to the call of a nation wishing us to remember its violence in carefully prescribed terms.

I don't know if Britain – being the nation it was in 1919 – had any other choice than to create a memorial like the Cenotaph. There is, of course, something inherently monstrous about violence, especially about violence on the scale of the Great War, precisely because it is predicated on denying another (indeed, 'the other') the full recognition of selfhood. Anthropologists have been telling us for a century that the violent, animal and animistic dimensions of ourselves will always be ritualised and codified in such a way that we can 'live' with them.[15] Without such sublimations, community and society cannot hope to flourish and survive. The Cenotaph is one way that a community hides the truth of its violence from itself. It is as crude and as sophisticated as the way flowers, and strong-fragranced lilies in particular, have become reactions to and symbolic of death. At one level, flowers can seem like nothing more than a practical response to the corruption of death in a pre-modern age – the need to cover up the fragrance of death's reality. They are also a prophylactic, a means of insulating us from the thing we fear or are threatened by. Ultimately, because they're such an effective sign, ironically they make us more mindful of what we would hide. They direct us towards the thing we fear. Thus, at a banal level, my mother's fear of receiving lilies – simply because they are 'for funerals' and death.

Perhaps, in the end, my fascination with the Cenotaph comes down to the way it both mediates and points towards our civilisation's violence. Perhaps that's why it keeps calling me and millions of others back – because it is our community's way of trying to make the incommensurate manageable. It is all we have in common. And ironically it cannot 'cover up' or 'hold' the violence – in seeking to reduce the loss of nearly a million to the understatement of a simple empty tomb, the (unavoidable?) callousness of the State is exposed and amplified. 'The Glorious Dead' is written upon it. It is the curse of the living, perhaps, to betray the dead, glorious or otherwise.

Yet, perhaps, you cannot keep the missing and the dead down for long. They will not rest. They will find other means to rise. Perhaps they have risen in the noise which now surrounds the Cenotaph. The noise provides a greater service for the dead than the silence of Remembrance Sunday. For it is the alternative narrative of radicals like the Gerzs reasserting itself. Rather than the noise being an unavoidable symptom of our forgetting of the lost, it is an invitation to commitment. We are being invited to forget our totemish obsession with fixed memorials; it is the totems themselves that will be forgotten.

CHAPTER TWO

'A Chapel' – Did the Great War leave God 'Hanging on the old barbed wire...'?[1]

*'The ancient churches, where the flags of the regiments
have been treasured, and whose walls will carry many
names of comrades sleeping on the battlefields or
beneath the ocean, will seem natural homes of religion
to the soldiers and sailors returning at last from war. A
new link between the Church and the nation will have
been forged in the furnace of affliction.'[2]*

In Manchester Cathedral there is, in the north-east corner, a large rectangular chapel. The focal point is a stained glass window in the east wall, a vast arch of red, orange and yellow glass that suggests flames and destruction. On the altar frontal beneath it and completing the fire motif is a phoenix. This window emerged from the ashes of a later conflict than the one which preoccupies this book. In the Manchester Blitz of 1940 the cathedral was bombed and burned. The Fire Window commemorates both the long nights of destruction, but also the resurrection out of the flames. The window is set in a place now known as The Regiment Chapel.

The Regiment Chapel commemorates, remembers and celebrates the service of The Duke of Lancaster Regiment and its precursors, including the Manchester Regiment. From the walls hang flags and battle honours, heavy with the conflicts of the twentieth century, among them Mons, Ypres, the Somme and Cambrai. Along the north edge are sturdy wooden display cases full of weighty books of remembrance. The pages are weighed down with the names of the fallen. On alternate Wednesdays, there is a simple service called 'The Turning of the Leaves', when the pages of the books are turned over. These are pages thick with memory, ritualised into manageable remembrance.

It is troubling to think about how the Church of England was complicit in the way the Great War was prosecuted. Elie Halévy notes how in the Great War state control of thought took two forms: the negative, aimed at suppressing the opinion deemed contrary to the national interest, and the positive appropriately termed 'the organisation of enthusiasm'. The Church of England was very much part of the latter. Indeed, until the formation of a department of information in 1917, propaganda was very much the business of private initiative. As Albert Marrin, who chronicles how the Great War was the last European holy war, argues, 'Convinced of the righteousness of England's cause, and believing that Christianity was concerned as much with the discharge of civic responsibilities as with the religious life, patriotic clergymen resolved to do their "bit" for King and Country.'[3] The consistent refrain of diocesan conferences and parish meetings was that the Church of England had a dual role – servant of God and servant of state. As servant of God, the Church of England provided huge amounts of practical humanitarian support to both needy soldiers at the front and their families at home, as well as supplying chaplains and distributing mind-bogglingly large number of Bibles and religious tracts. It is a token of how far we have changed as a society that we can neither quite imagine prosecuting a conflict on the scale of the Great War nor conceive of a church that might generate that level of scriptural provision. I have a copy of the New Testament that was supplied to my grandad Sam, along with millions of other soldiers. One cannot quite imagine these little booklets would be welcomed by today's troops let alone provided.[4] But that is nothing compared to the shattering participation the church played in recruitment drives and propaganda for the war. Truly, with far too few exceptions,[5] the Church of England was an agent of the mobilised state, a recruiting sergeant for destruction.

The Bishop of London, the Worcestershire-born Arthur Winnington-Ingram remains the single most notorious figure among the clergy active as recruiters for war, yet as Marrin reminds us again and again, there was no shortage of clerics willing to preach for the patriotic cause. Rev. Richard Huggard, Vicar of St John's Barnsley claimed to have personally enlisted two thousand men. The Rev. A.W. Gough, Vicar of Brompton and Prebendary of St Paul's suggested that every Englishman worthy of the name should don with pride the khaki uniform, 'the festal garment which God is offering us today, which he is insisting that we put on.' Equally the Rev. James Bent of Salford Dock Mission dared to claim that 'the most encouraging feature to all Christians is the glorious fact that thousands of men are finding even in the trenches a sanctuary, a very Bethel'. Given what I shall say in a later chapter about the experience of the Salford and Trafford Pals Battalions at the Somme – battalions Bent may have helped recruit – it is hard not to respond by saying that the only thing they found was death.

Winnington-Ingram – a man who loved to throw on a uniform and hang around recruiting rallies – boasted of having been thanked officially by the War Office for having added ten thousand men to the fighting forces of the crown; soon thereafter a grateful king appointed him KCVO. His famous sermon 'A Call To Arms' was credited for inducing two brigades to go overseas. Marrin concludes, 'It should also be noted that the Hensley Hensons, the Paul Bulls and the Winnington-Ingrams were experienced preachers who had spent years in refining their techniques and studying their listeners. They were adept at using emotive words, and a few of their recruiting speeches, embellishing with a phraseology calculated to appeal simultaneously to religious feelings, love of country, and the emotions are masterpieces of the salesman's art.'[6]

Much of the behaviour of the Church of England both at home and on and near the front line reminds us of how very much it was the State Religion, caught up in interests often tangentially of interest to serving men. If, for a moment, we set aside its recruiting role and even accept that the war was being fought for good ends and for winnable goals, too often the official church at the front, in the shape of the Chaplain, let down the men. There are, indeed, justly famous stories of the likes of Geoffrey Studdert Kennedy aka 'Woodbine Willie' distributing comfort to soldiers in the front line, but most remember the Chaplain as a distant, formal figure.[7] This was, in many cases, not their fault. Unlike their Roman Catholic counterparts – who were expected to be in the front line, even taking part in offensives in order to offer the grace of Extreme Unction – Anglican chaplains were held back, sometimes in protest. In a move almost calculated to widen the often extraordinary social gap between chaplain and men, if a chaplain wanted to go into no-man's-land to act as a stretcher bearer, he had to disobey the notorious standing order against Church of England chaplains going forward of Brigade HQ. For every P.B. 'Tubby' Clayton – who set up that impressive place of support, Talbot House, aka Toc H, in the grim staging-post Poperinghe – there was the class-bound padre unable to connect with men many of whom had only the vaguest comprehension of the ministrations of the Anglican Church.

However, the most resented aspect of church-associated life for the common soldier was monthly Compulsory Church Parade. This was, in the mind of many, just another inspection and the preaching was a point of irritation. At least the likes of Winnington-Ingram had developed an interesting style; those who presided over the parades seemed intent on boredom and the deathly dull.[8] My Grandad Sam spent part of his service in the Middle East and Marrin's image is evocative: 'One can imagine hundreds of sweating men, their buttons shining in the Mesopotamian sun fidgeting as the padre preached interminably on the death of Socrates, the cruise of the Argo or the commutation of tithes.' Grandad Sam was, like many of his generation, a conventional Anglican. I have a copy of Thomas à Kempis' *The Imitation of Christ* given to him at confirmation. But he rarely darkened the door of a church after the war, except to marry or at death. There will be myriad reasons for his absence. The Church had never had great success at retaining its youth. At the turn of the century, three out of four children were, according to Alan Wilkinson, Sunday School attendees, but there is little evidence that this was born out in regular adult attendance. Leading churchmen of the day, including Charles Gore, noted how disconnected the Church of England was from the working classes. Working class men like Sam were perhaps never destined to find their happy home in church, but I find it difficult to resist the notion that his experience in foreign fields broke such ties he'd known.

For whom was the God proclaimed by the Church? And what account of suffering was it able to give? As Wilkinson suggests, 'God speaks to the Church through the world, as well as to the world through the Church ... In this period, that Word emerged more authentically from the prose and poetry of Siegfried Sassoon and Wilfred Owen than it did, say, from the sermons of Winnington-Ingram.'[9] However, it's worth noting that the words of the poets were not necessarily representative of the feelings of the common soldier. Equally, like much art, I'm inclined to say they 'reached ahead', helping others comprehend the madness. If the poets' words did not determine how the future would see the past, they made a decisive contribution to shaping future generations' perception of it. The artist, like a soldier advancing into no-man's-land, goes ahead, searching for the trap, the snare, the tinkle of wire that signals the gap between doom and continued life. Notoriously, Winnington-Ingram preached, in St Paul's Cathedral on 9 August 1914, that if a pagan poet could proclaim, 'Dulce et decorum est pro patria mori,' 'with how much more conviction should a Christian parent say the same?' At that point – pre-slaughter –

such sentiments were perhaps comprehensible and commonplace. After Loos and especially the Somme, fewer expressed the glory of death – for country or otherwise.

At the front, the chaplain's job was often impossible. For soldiers – who'd perhaps scraped the remains of pals up into a sandbag – often found the chaplains' talk of the weightiness of death and the 'resurrection of the body' lightweight. At home, the presence of death and bereavement on an industrial scale led to a rediscovery of 'Catholic' practices of praying for the dead. Indeed, 1917 signalled the publication of an authorised prayer for the departed. At or near the front, soldiers came across crucifixes, often for the first time. A section of the Somme was called 'Calvary Corner' because of the Calvary which stood there. The notion of redemption by the shedding of blood, or a national and personal crucifixion as a place of purgation and redemption found purchase in some quarters. In 1915, the chaplain Fr Paul Bull preached on Hebrews 12.1: 'After a year of crucifixion our Nation answers with unflinching resolution, "To the last drop of our blood."' Yet others felt like the war-weary Tommy who, on seeing a battlefield Calvary, said 'Who was he anyway? I bet I've suffered more than he ever did.'

As I flick through Brian Gardner's famous anthology of Great War poetry *Up the Line to Death*, page after page of moderate verse greets me – so many uneven poems about valour and glory. Blunden and Sassoon today fail to engage me. I am only moderately involved with John Peale Bishop's 'In the Dordogne'. Even Rosenberg, brilliant Isaac Rosenberg, fails to grab me. I flick on to be stopped, arrested even, by Wilfred Owen. And I ask myself, 'Why? Why this poetry?' And part of the answer I sense is to do with the fact that I'm essentially conventional and not very imaginative. Part of the answer lies in Owen's impact on my fourteen-year-old self. After being forced to study Browning's 'My Last Duchess' and Arnold's 'Dover Beach', Owen simply crackled with energy. His imagery startled me with its immediacy. The empathy, the bitterness, and the pity speak. For a while Browning and Arnold didn't stand a chance. And though he doesn't rank so high in my adult estimation of poets,[10] Owen is the reason I study and try to write poetry today.

But there is another reason I stop at Owen today and it's to do with his wider cultural impact. It's his poetry, more than any other, which determines how most British people see the Great War in particular and war in general. His poetry anticipated how, on one level, the War would be remembered. Writing in 1917–18 he wrote how the future would see the past. Geoff Dyer notes how in 1914 the eleven-year-old Eric Blair, aka George Orwell, could write a heartfelt poem – 'Awake, young men of England' – relying entirely on the received sentiment of the martial verse tradition; equally, today, an eleven-year-old could write in a heartfelt way about the 'horror of war' whilst relying entirely on received sentiment. This is, of course, not to deny that the Great War or any war isn't horrific, but rather to state that most of our response to war is as conditioned. In some respects, Owen's verse (along with Sassoon's) make 'anti-war' poetry as unthinking and pre-conditioned as Brooke's 'begloried sonnets' (as Isaac Rosenberg put it) were conditioned by pre-war martial verse. The contingent nature of this is surely a salutary reminder that an 'anti-war' stance – even for those claiming religious warrant for it – is no given.

Wilfred Owen's name is found in Manchester Cathedral's Regiment Chapel. He was a 2nd Lieutenant in the 2nd Manchesters and was gazetted for the MC:

2nd Lt, Wilfred Edward Salter Owen, 5th Bn. Manch. R., T.F., attd. 2nd Bn. For conspicuous gallantry and devotion to duty in the attack on the Fonsomme Line on October 1st/2nd, 1918. On the company commander becoming a casualty, he assumed command and showed fine leadership and resisted a heavy counter-attack. He personally manipulated a captured enemy machine gun from an isolated position and inflicted considerable losses on the enemy. Throughout he behaved most gallantly. On 4th November 1918, he was killed whilst attempting to traverse the Sambre Canal.

It is worth noting, though not overstressing, that Wilfred Owen at one time considered becoming an Anglican priest. Between 1911 and 1913 he worked as lay assistant to the vicar of Dunsden. This 'deepened his social awareness and compassion as he visited the poor of the parish, but it also destroyed the evangelical faith he had inherited from his mother.'[11] As Alan Wilkinson argues, 'The majority of his war poems show him testing biblical and Christian images and doctrines to see whether they will bear the weight of the increasing revulsion he felt against the slaughter.'[12] If the Somme provides the great ironic moment in the public life of the war, Owen's poetry and life represent the literary archetype for the Great War's ironic assault. In order to appreciate this we should remember that in 1914, H. C. Beeching, the literary Dean of Norwich, could say without embarrassment that war gave the poet the opportunity to celebrate patriotism, love of freedom and heroic exploits; there was 'no more honourable service' than that of the poet in wartime. Owen's mature poetry underlines this latter point, but in quite a different way to that which Beeching imagined.

Owen was not a religious poet; his subject, as he famously put it, was 'War and the pity of War. The poetry is in the pity'. And yet his poetry and his letters play with and push against biblical images and theological concepts; he is profoundly aware of God and Christ. And yet this wrestling with God is imbued with rich irony and ambivalence. It is as if he is trying to make sense of an abridged or compromised God for times of abridged hope, for a place of compromise. A God who can make a kind of home in an ironic world. Owen discovers a God both greater and lesser than he imagined. In one of his letters, he suggests,

Christ is literally in no man's land. There men often hear His voice: Greater love hath no man than this, that a man lay down his life – for a friend. Is it spoken in English only and in French? I do not believe so. Thus you see how pure Christianity will not fit in with

pure patriotism … Christians have deliberately cut some of the main teaching of their code.[13]

Owen, then, found himself drawn close to Christ in his passion though he expresses this closeness with irony:

For 14 hours yesterday I was at work – teaching Christ to lift his cross by numbers, and how to adjust his crown; and not to imagine he thirsts until after the last halt; I attended his Supper to see that there were no complaints; and inspected his feet to see that they should be worthy of the nails. I see to it that he is dumb and stands to attention before his accusers. With a piece of silver I buy him every day, and with maps I make him familiar with the topography of Golgotha.[14]

The contrast with the God/Christ of the Anglican churchmen *cum* recruiting sergeants is striking. Theirs typically reflects the muscularity and presumed masculinity of their class. As Modris Eksteins strikingly puts it, 'Clergymen dressed Jesus in khaki and had him firing machine-guns.'[15] Their god is one that echoes through the martial fair-play of the poetry of Sir Henry Newbolt in his most famous poem, 'Vitai Lampada', which imagines a soldier bringing the virtues of his school and sport, specifically cricket, into the battlefield:

> *The river of death has brimmed his banks,*
> *And England's far, and Honour a name,*
> *But the voice of a schoolboy rallies the ranks:*
> *'Play up! play up! and play the game!'*

Newbolt was a lifelong friend of Douglas Haig, the British army commander from 1916 till the end of the war. They'd met at Clifton College whose cricket field provides the location for the first stanza of 'Vitai'. As Paul Fussell quotes, 'Much later Newbolt wrote, "When I looked into Douglas Haig I saw what is really great – perfect acceptance, which means perfect faith.'"[16] The Establishment, of which the Church of England was part, celebrated what Patrick Howarth has called, 'homo newboltiensis': the man who is stoic, honourable, brave, loyal and a little unimaginative.

The god of the Anglican recruiting sergeants is the patriarchal god, shaped in their own image and inherited from decades of English imperial confidence and growth. As Wilkinson puts it, 'The public schools had taught their pupils patriotism, self-sacrifice, athleticism, Spartan habits and discipline in the name of the "The Manliness of Christ" (the title of a book by Thomas Hughes published in 1876).'[17] The Episcopal and clerical recruiting sergeants of 1914 were part of a class and culture that comprehended the old truth that son inherited from father in the fullness of time if the son was faithful to his elder. For the elder was, ultimately, to be trusted. The evidence for this lay in one hundred years of relative peace in which England's power had grown to its zenith.

But if the naive and smug overconfidence of a proprietary church convinced of its righteousness and goodness is distasteful to both modern religious and secular tastes, it is childish not to appreciate the impact of this comfortable faith on the Church. If there were many a clerical equivalent of the bumptious Colonel Blimp, the bright boys of the church were not afraid to bleed for their beliefs. As Bob Holman notes, 'by the end of the war there were 3,475 [chaplains].'[18] By the end of the war, 172 chaplains lay dead, of which 88 were Anglican. Four received the Victoria Cross. Furthermore, it is sobering to examine the statistics for ordinands who joined up and the impact on the clerical leadership for the church post-war. In 1914 there were 1274 students enrolled in 32 Anglican theological colleges. Nearly 400 withdrew immediately. This represented a massive hit to a church which expected 600 ordinations a year. Ordinations then fell steadily during the war, from 610 in (effectively pre-war) 1914 to 161 in 1919, the last figure representing a post-war increase over 114 in 1918. In a classic piece of Anglican understatement, Wilkinson claims that 'The church would miss this "lost generation" of priests for decades to come.'[19] Other Anglican activities suffered massively as well. By 1915, 2700 Church of England elementary school teachers had joined up. Many never returned to their pre-war tasks.

The extent to which the Great War severed the Gordian Knot between Church and the Nation's ready affections is moot. However, as the war progressed one thing became increasingly clear: that for all the complex and sometimes brilliant work wrought by chaplains and volunteers at or near the front line, the Church of England had got itself into a media mess at home. At the heart of this was the question of whether an ordained man could be a combatant in the armed forces. There was considerable handwringing from the top down. In a private letter to the Bishop of Salisbury in 1914, the Archbishop of Canterbury, Randall Davidson wrote: 'I do not believe that an ordained man ought to be combatant in the army ... I do not of course say that this should be applicable in the moment of supremest urgency in the Nation's life, or if the country were invaded, or the Man's parish being attacked.' Since at least the Middle Ages, canon law had forbidden clerics to take up arms or engage in war (though this hadn't prevented warrior-clerics from wielding a club rather than an edged weapon or, on occasions, commanding large armies).

Until the Derby Scheme's findings were known in early 1916,[20] clergy exemption was based more on traditional practice than the law of the land. The issue hit 'pay-dirt', of course, when clergy sought to embarrass the craven and the cowardly to join up, but had exemptions from service themselves. Winnington-Ingram, along with the bishops of Carlisle, Chester and Manchester declared a ban, effective on 18 June 1916, on ordinations for men in condition to serve. Marrin concludes, 'There was no general outcry (about clergy exemption) until the clergy of all denominations were excused from attesting under the Derby Scheme, and in 1916 exempted from the Military Service Act. At this point the mood changed perceptibly, organised religion as a whole, and the Church of England in particular, becoming the target for wholesale abuse.'[21] It wasn't until April 1918, in the light of the terror spread by the success of the German Spring Offensive (which at one point saw the Germans closing in on Paris) that the clergy exemption was seen fit to be removed. (Along with military age lifted from 41 to 50.) The Archbishop of Canterbury immediately gave his blessing to the new Military Service Bill. However, by mid-April the decision to include clergy was reversed on the back of fears of another Irish rebellion if Roman Catholic priests were conscripted.

For Wilfred Owen, the War expanded his vision of God beyond the conventional Evangelicalism of his upbringing: 'I have heard cadences of harps not audible to Sankey, but which were strung by God ... there is a point where prayer is indistinguishable from blasphemy. There is also a point where blasphemy is indistinguishable from prayer.'[22] Perhaps in this single sentence, Owen captures the weightlessness of much of what might be called the 'Church-ianity' offered by the Edwardian patriarchal Anglicanism of the Great War. For surely in times of extremis – and what was the Great War if not a time of extremis? – the blunt, the blasphemous and the desperate can speak more powerfully than carefully crafted words.

Siegfried Sassoon's poem 'Attack!' closes with the line, 'O Jesus, make it stop!' Surely, those words (with the addition of suitable expletives) are much nearer to the kind of language substantial enough to take the weight of prayer in extremis. Perhaps these have been the words of countless people down the centuries caught in situations of intense need where our usual pious formulations seem as substantial as the promises of a tyrant. Sassoon wrote those words as the closing line of a poem about a trench attack in a now ancient war; yet because they were generated out of experience in extremis, they retain the power and substance to speak into human extremes. I do not think that it's cheap to say that one does not have to have experienced being shelled on the Western Front, or in Bosnia, Afghanistan or Syria, to know times when, as Sassoon's poem also states, 'hope, with furtive eyes and grappling fists, flounders in mud' and the only prayerful Christian response is 'O Jesus, make it stop!'

When Owen claims, 'there is a point where prayer is indistinguishable from blasphemy. There is also a point where blasphemy is indistinguishable from prayer' he is suggesting that in some extreme circumstances the sacred and profane meet and embrace. This embrace is often a wordless cry. Sassoon's 'O Jesus, make it stop!' gives some words for that cry. Its direct, terse nature makes it almost an expletive, a prayerful 'f-word'. Indeed, the 'O Jesus' has both the feel of a petition and the edge of the modern-day usage heard every day on our streets as a throwaway expletive. To try to offer to God anything more nuanced in times of abject pain, terror or fear, I sense would be an attempt to soften reality. The dreadfulness of pain and the dignity of the sufferer demand words as immediate and as fierce as Sassoon gives us. Sometimes the only suitable prayer is blasphemy; we dishonour God and reality if we do not offer up words of blasphemy and cursing. For, although the psalms and the patterns of our conventional prayers can bring comfort and encouragement, indeed speak deeply into our need, there are places beyond ready comfort. There are places which are experienced as both tragedy and utter barrenness, and perhaps can only be appropriately experienced as such. Sometimes the psalms meet our needs in those places and sometimes they are not enough.

The philosopher Gillian Rose famously uses Staretz Silouan's 'keep your mind in hell and do not despair' as the epigraph for her autobiography.[23] This phrase underlined Rose's determination to keep face-to-face with reality, especially as she faced death from cancer. She was determined not to take flight into a comforting vision of wholeness any more than she was prepared to be reduced to bitter atomistic selfishness by her disease. Her commitment was a profound statement on God's invitation to be and become our true selves. This is so often a place of abiding darkness, seeking comprehension. As Jon Stallworthy puts it rather brilliantly, 'Orpheus, the pagan saint of poets, went through hell and came back singing. In twentieth-century mythology, the singer wears a steel helmet and makes his descent 'down some profound dull tunnel' in the stinking mud of the Western Front. For most readers of English poetry, the face under the helmet is that of Wilfred Owen.'[24]

The Anglican Church was – understandably – obsessed about how it could exercise its place as State Religion in the midst of the greatest conflict of all time. If it fell foul of the comfortable god it had made for itself, perhaps Owen's verse gives us glimpses of a god both big enough and small enough for the world the Great War inaugurated. For, if Owen did not, in situ, speak for the soldiers and people with whom he served (the likes of my grandfathers), he anticipated how the post-war world would begin to see itself. For the Anglican Church in 1914 was not fit for what was to come. Perhaps, no institution was. The Church of England in 1914 was made for more fertile and static times.[25] Its message was shaped in the corridors of power and comfort and service to the State. Indeed, the Church of England in 1914 was confident in its place within the Establishment in ways we cannot quite comprehend now. Its fundamental message was grounded in the muscular belief that through sheer courage, endurance and Christian manliness, hope can overcome evil times. Its message was: If you will only endure this time, we shall return to sunlit uplands, essentially unchanged – a land of plenty and hope and glory, where in time the young shall inherit the good things from the old. But the War inaugurated a new world – a world of, what Paul Fussell labelled, 'abridged hope'. Or, if it did not quite inaugurate it, it rehearsed it in such a way that no one would ever quite forget the lesson. This was a world shaped by mistrust, endlessly deflated expectations, of failed 'pushes' and 'offensives', of countless ironies and disappointments.

If the Church of England continued to articulate a Patriarchal God throughout the war (and perhaps still does to this day), Owen offers glimpses of something else. In his lesser-known poem 'The Parable of the Old Man and the Young' (a retelling of the Abraham and Isaac myth), Owen signifies the death of patriarchal society and the God to which it is beholden. Beginning on familiar territory ('So Abram rose, and clave the wood, and went,/And took the fire with him, and knife.'), the poem unfolds into a nightmarish trench-based scene ('Then Abram bound the youth with belts and straps,/And builded parapets and trenches there,/And stretched forth the knife to slay his son.'). As in the Biblical story, an Angel intervenes and invites Abram to 'Lay not thy hand upon the lad' and sacrifice 'the Ram of Pride instead'. The conclusion of the poem is devastating in its simple condemnation of the 'Good Father' principle: 'But the old man would not so, but slew his son,/And half the seed of Europe, one by one.'[26]

Pat Barker, in the first of her *Regeneration* trilogy (in which she fictionalises the encounter between Sassoon and Owen at Craiglockart Hospital in 1917) takes up this theme. She has the (real-life) psychiatrist W.H.R. Rivers put a further gloss on the myth underlining Owen's poem. Whilst attending a church service he looks at the east window. Beneath a crucifixion scene is a representation of the Abraham and Isaac story. With an anthropologist's eyes, Rivers sees these two scenes (Crucifixion and Abraham/Isaac) as 'obvious choices'. These are, he thinks, 'the two bloody bargains on which a civilisation claims to be based.' Indeed, '*The* bargain, Rivers thought, looking at Abraham and Isaac. The one on which all patriarchal societies are founded.' The essence of that bargain he suggests is, 'If you, who are young and strong, will obey me, who am old and weak, even to the extent of being prepared to sacrifice your life, then in the course of time you will peacefully inherit, and be able to exact the same obedience from your sons.' Yet, as is clear to Rivers, in Flanders and Picardy, the old were sending off the young in breach of that bargain.[27]

Arguably, the patriarchal God died on the Somme, at Ypres and Passchendaele. He – like so many – was left 'hanging on the old barbed wire'. Unlike the poor lads on both sides who went over the top, he perhaps hangs there still. The Churches will not let him go. What is for sure is that in our time the traditional churches are in crisis. I do not know if this is because churches like my own, the Church of England, have yet to move on from this dead, male-centric God. I suspect it may be one reason among many. The reasons for the masses no longer coming to church (if they ever did) are complex and multiform. I am inclined to leave that assessment to sociologists of religion. What is clear is that the patriarchal God could not – in the light of years of slaughter – quite hold the weight of expectations. Ultimately, it proved to be a hapless, unreliable 'idol'.

What is psychologically intriguing is how difficult it is to lay the patriarchal idol down. Perhaps that is why the English church retains such affection for it. Perhaps that is why I feel a kind of regret that he is 'dead'. I'm mostly glad the English patriarchal God is dying. I regret that it happened in the way it did in the shit-pit that was the Western Front. And, yet, within me remains a patriarchal remnant. I have not yet properly let patriarchy go. And that part of me wishes he'd never died. For there is something comforting in the myth it gestures towards – that the young can trust the old, for the old are wise and comprehend the world; that the men who have lived long and been shaped to rule have acquired wisdom in such a way that they shall pass it down to those to come; that the world is essentially unchanging and shall be as it always has been; that those who rule do so because they were born to rule and/or have acquired wisdom to do so, and so on. No matter who gets excluded from this picture – women, the poor, the queer, people of colour, etc. – it is 'feudal-pastoral' reified as the Story of God. And while it represents a world which readily excludes all sorts of narratives, at least offered a picture that – despite its limits – countless souls have committed themselves to.

Christianity – especially in its post-Constantinian co-option as 'state' or 'imperial' religion – has always run the risk of becoming a hand-maiden of power and authority. It does not have to be so. Early Christianity was fundamentally pacific. At the heart of its story was a proclamation – via some of the Hebraic prophets, notably Deutero-Isaiah – of Yahweh as reconciling and loving. In early Christianity, the anointed saviour was less a king or warrior;

still less Christ Pantocrator, the imperial dispenser of justice. He was a peasant, a nobody, condemned to death on an imperial means of torture. He was a prophet whose 'good news' disrupts and challenges comfortable assumptions and often doesn't look much like 'goodness' or 'news'. In suggesting that Jesus was an embodiment of God, early Christianity united itself to insights of Second Isaiah: that suffering (of Israel or of Christ) was not a sign of guiltiness or cause for resentment of YHWH, but a new revelation of the divine nature. It indicated God's solidarity with the victim, not the powerful. It showed that God – and being faithful to him – was not about success and blessing traditionally shown in the projection of power and conquest. It revealed that suffering was not about punishment of vice and sin, but the result of human scheming and hubris. YHWH/God no longer needed to be co-opted for the schemes of men; the call was to live differently, seeking to be faithful to God's promises.

For the ignominious death of Christ, most of all, was not about his unrighteousness but a result of human choices (most especially power elites threatened by his faithfulness). At a profound level, early Christianity – as a statement of Divine Love – was an act of resistance to the belief that God is definitively to be found in work of the successful, the powerful and their manoeuvring, including the prosecution of war. As the psychologist and historian Sue Mansfield puts it, 'From [the perspective of early and mystic Christianity], war is simply one of the side effects of human error, a sign that humans' separation from their true nature has not been overcome ... once God is understood as love, war ceases to have any mythological meaning or transcendent imperative, since it imitates no divine gesture.'[28] Yet, how difficult did the Anglican leaders of 1914 find it to leave behind their imperial, patriarchal visions of God? The fanatical, crusading behaviour of the Church in the Great War is not the least of arguments against too close a relationship between Church and State.[29]

Who is the God, then, which emerges out of broken myth? What God does Owen show us in a world where blasphemy is prayer? What kind of God will do for ironic times? And what kind of Christian 'man' will bear 'his' image? Henry Newbolt, who was so key in poetically representing a public school version of Christian manliness, was not impressed with the Owens and Sassoons. He wrote, 'Owen and the rest of the broken men rail at the Old Men who sent the young to die: they have suffered cruelly, but in the nerves and not the heart – they haven't experience or imagination to know the extreme human agony.'[30] I suspect most of us would disagree and argue that we need to travel with Owen to the places of passion and crucifixion. Perhaps we need to wrestle with ambiguity. Part of the puzzle and interest of Owen was that he wrestled with the pacific utterances of Jesus and yet never became a pacifist. He was a divided self. At one point he asks, 'And am I not myself a conscientious objector with a very seared conscience?'[31] He could write to his mother, 'shells made by women in Birmingham are at this moment burying little children alive not very far from here'[32] and yet be glad to be recommended for a Military Cross.

Although I might draw my ambiguities in different places, I identify with Owen's wrestling and sense that this 'divided self' is part of the essence of modern living. Despite my attraction to pre-Constantinian Christianities and their enactment of 'the pacific God', I'm not sure I'm clear-minded enough to 'lay down' my respect for those willing to serve, to fight. It is a theme I return to, again and again, in different forms: my suspicion of 'purity' and 'holiness' as a kind of focused, occasionally monomaniacal, surety about who God is or what Christianity 'is'. As if God and religion might readily be redacted out of context and history. 'God Abridged', as it were. But this lack of conviction is perhaps what makes me a bad theologian (if an honest one). As for Owen, he died on 4 November 1918. As if to offer the Great War its final ironic vignette, the telegram telling Owen's parents of his death on 4 November 1918 arrived one hour after the armistice had been signed. A family's hope abridged to absence.

CHAPTER THREE

'A Street Memorial' – What exactly was 'lost' in the catastrophe of 'The Somme'?

'See that little stream – we could walk to it in two minutes. It took the British a month to walk it – a whole empire walking very slowly, dying in front and pushing forward behind. And another empire walking very slowly backwards a few inches a day, leaving the dead like a million bloody rugs.... This took religion and years of plenty and tremendous sureties and the exact relation between the classes...this land here cost twenty lives a foot that summer.'[1]

Of all the startling, unexpected memorials to the Great War I've come across, the one on Trafford Grove trumps them all. Trafford Grove, in Stretford, Manchester, is a curious terrace of back-to-backs saved from demolition in the 1990s because of their peculiarity. For in a city full of terraces, Trafford Grove is unusual in that each little house has a small front yard garden. The 'road' itself comprises a cobbled walkway. As one walks down it, especially at twilight in the dim street lights, one could swear you still hear the voices of the early twentieth century on the breeze – the coarse banter of the labourers who found a home here, the jokes of their wives and the tip-tap of children's clogs. One can almost smell the scent of fish and chips on the breeze. And, not least among its peculiarities, halfway down, attached to the side of a house is a neat, faded hand-finished plaque. Originally erected just after the War, it holds the names of those men from the street who fought and died in it. In total, there are sixty names, a roll of honour that includes both those who died and those who, more or less, survived. I lived on this street as a curate. When the vicar invited me to go look at the property they'd found me I liked it. Discovering the roll of honour ensured that I went to live there.

The existence of other such rolls of honour, especially in the North, is a testimony to the truth that, despite Scott Fitzgerald's talk of empires moving forward and back like chess pieces, the Great War was a people's war, a civilian's war, a local war. Whole streets and communities joined *en masse*, moved by the call of neighbour, of Country and King. And if the latter two did not hold the power many think they did, certainly the desire to be with one's mates and not be left out, did. Trafford Grove's roll of honour is a testimony not only to the urge to remember the fallen, but to the pride that was felt. It is, among other things, a reminder that Britain was still a great imperial power at the end of the war – that the people, dirt poor as they might have been, had internalised the way in which the imperial mind seeks to solemnise and ritualise the offerings that have been slaughtered on its table. The roll of honour is two feet by four, covered with flags at the top and two lions at the base. The names are hand written, including a name clearly added at a later date and – whatever colour it was originally – is now a very faded blue. Since the upsurge of interest in remembrance since the mid-1990s, it receives its wreath of poppies on Armistice Day. If it was created out of the will to remember it was also generated out of pride and trust in who they were – poor, yes, but those who had served and who could take pride in their national identity in an unalloyed way. Later generations, fully receiving the fruits of abridged hope, more committed to scepticism and questioning the place of identity and imperial power had no such luxury.

The Battle of the Somme is, in the English mind, the meeting point of the impossible demands of empire and the local; between civilian and military; between the fragility of the human body and sheer destructive power. It was the place Grandad Bert mentioned once or twice and it was where he was wounded for the first time. If Passchendaele provides popular memory with its key images of the war – mud, filth, pointlessness – the Somme was, in so many ways, the end of all things. The end of the Empire, though it did not realise it yet; the end of the traditional feudal class system, though it stuttered on for a few years and, in our collective imagination, the end of innocence, even if that innocence had already been shattered at First Ypres or Arras. Even if that innocence had always been a falsehood. Dick Diver, the protagonist in F. Scott Fitzgerald's *Tender is the Night*, captures a profound truth, certainly about Britain after the Great War, in the passage I quote: 'No European will ever do that again in this generation ... this western-front business couldn't be done again, not for a long time. The young men think they could do it but they couldn't. They could fight the first Marne again but not this.'

I am aware that the terrain of the Somme has been subject to relentless intellectual blasting. Its cultural map is as shattered and twisted as the physical terrain. Unlike the physical terrain, at a cultural level it has not been allowed to grow new grass, to recover. At the same time, its cultural meaning is, like the physical space, in danger of being memorialised in particular ways. But I must talk about it, not only because it has, for the British, become in myth *the* satire of the war, but also because it was the event that took my grandfathers to the centre of the satire. They were part of Kitchener's great volunteer army, the civilian-soldiers who experienced the end of the world in those definitive months of 1916. Though my grandfathers were not killed, though they may not have been physically injured, they became casualties. They were not lost, but they joined the ranks of the missing of the Somme.

The grand facts about the so-called Battle[2] of the Somme and, especially, its first day (1 July 1916) are well known. I do not propose to rehearse them all here. However, within its grand and terrible satire of circumstance it is worth highlighting a few particulars which mark out its terrific irony. The site of the disaster, as John Keegan notes, 'had not been contested since the first weeks of the war ... the Germans had profited from the peace in which they had been left since 1914 to construct the strongest position on the Western Front.'[3] Their dugouts were impervious to even the most powerful British shells. The British trenches, recently vacated by the French, were in a poor state. And, then, we have the soldiers – the likes of my grandfathers, the agricultural and factory hands, the clerks and tradesmen. The army of the Somme (the 4th Army) was for the most part, a 'Kitchener' Army, so-named after the recently-dead Secretary for War[4] who had asked for 100,000 volunteers in 1914 and got ten times that number. This was a citizen army, many of whose battalions were 'Pals' or 'Chums' formations comprised of work colleagues and friends who'd 'joined together and served together'. Many died together.[5] Less than half a mile from my old house on Trafford Grove lie the former docks and factories of Manchester, Salford and Trafford. From these cramped districts three battalions of Lancashire Fusiliers were recruited. On 1 July, they lost 41 officers and 942 men.[6] Like my grandfathers, these were men whose motivation for enlistment ranged from the patriotic through to the fact the army offered three square meals a day through to the need not to be left out. The Somme was to be their first battle and they 'had no doubts in the High Command or in itself.'[7]

Hope of decisive victory among these formations pre-battle was incredibly high. An enormous bombardment, to last a week and consume one million shells, preceded the attack. However, so certain were Haig and most of his subordinates of the crushing effect the artillery would produce, that they had decided not to allow the inexperienced infantry to advance by the tried and tested means of 'fire and movement', when some lay down to cover with rifle volleys the advance of the rest, but to keep them moving forward upright and in straight lines.[8] In addition, troops were expected to carry sixty pounds of equipment across a mauled no-man's-land. Haig expected Bapaume, seven miles behind enemy lines, to be reached by the end of the first day of the battle.

However, 'the innocent army fully attained the knowledge of good and evil at the Somme on 1 July 1916. That moment, one of the most interesting in the whole long history of human disillusion, can stand as the type of all the ironic actions of the war.'[9] The weather heightened the irony, as in the summer of 1914. Siegfried Sassoon noted, 'On the first of July the weather, after an early morning mist, was of the kind commonly called heavenly.'[10] Fussell argues, in relation to a number of memoirs of that day that precisely what enables the memoirist, whether literary or vulgar, to remember is the application of an ironic structure which subsequent vision has laid over the events. So, for Charles Bricknall, a working-class private soldier, it is the contrast between his memory of the arrival of new soldiers who were 'all spick and span, buttons polished and the rest of it' in counterpoint to their slaughter that makes both the particular and the general memorable. The innocence of the 'sporting spirit'/'war as game' is definitively realised in the much-reported incident when Captain W.P. Nevill of the 8th East Surrey's provided footballs for his company to kick across no-man's-land during the Somme attack. As Captain Alfred Irwin reports, 'They went forward shouting with such energy, kicking the football ahead of them. But so quickly Nevill and his second in command were both killed plus his company sergeant-major.'[11]

But I didn't need to tell you that – so deep is the ironic structure of the Somme embedded in us, that you knew I would tell you that. The 'confidence' implicit in Nevill's men stands in contrast to the reality in a way that literature would consider crude or vulgar.[12] As the great memoirist Edmund Blunden put it, 'By the end of the day both sides had seen, in a sad scrawl of broken earth and murdered men, the answer to the question. No road. No thoroughfare. Neither race had won, nor could win, the War.

The War had won, and would go on winning.'[13] Of the 100,000 British soldiers in the attack, there had been 60,000 casualties, 20,000 of whom were killed. As even Niall Ferguson – a historian who powerfully and often convincingly questions the 'lions led by donkeys' myth – accepts, the extent of loss 'becomes clear when it is realised that the German defenders suffered only 8000.'[14] Some battalions simply ceased to exist.

'On 1 January 1917, Haig was elevated to the rank of Field Marshal, and on 17 March, Bapaume – one of the main first-day objectives of the Somme jump-off nine months before – was finally captured.'[15] It is the dynamics of hope abridged, whether in the particular micro- or general macro-satire of circumstance, that make the Somme haunt the memory. The Somme represents an archetype for 'abridged hope'; it represents and, in large measure, inaugurates a dominant mode of modern understanding – the ironic. This is a dominant story of our time. Ours is an age where commitment and trust and faith are treated as naive, suspicious and open to contempt. In a world come of age no one wants to be caught out and made a fool of. And on the evidence of the seeming profligacy of leaders during the Great War, rightly so.

There will be communities around the world – in Afghanistan, in Darfur, in Russia, in Poland – who know what it is for whole generations to disappear, for villages and towns to be effectively wiped off the map. Continental Europe has known, over the centuries, almost endless destruction from the devastation of the Thirty Years War through to the Holocaust of 1939–45. But in Britain, we cannot comprehend the shattering of ways of life and indeed whole communities except through the missing of the Somme. Yes, there will be those who argue that the Somme was, ultimately, a victory or placed in the perspective of the whole war, the British losses were not exceptional. There is – in purely military terms – a strong case for claiming that the Somme, along with Verdun, was the condition of victory in the West. German morale took a huge hit with the High Command realising that (without the vast reinforcements which ultimately arrived after the defeat of Russia) it could only fight a defensive war. There is a profound sense that given both the nature of the war and the British Army in 1916 – predominantly green, untested civilians in uniform – a battle like the Somme was necessary for it to become fit for purpose. The five months of the battle, from July through to November, ensured that in the final phase of the war, Britain actually possessed the best and most impressive fighting force.

In 1914 Britain was alone among the major combatants in having a professional army, comprised of the desperate, the poor and (occasionally) the posh, which, if designed for colonial warfare, were capable of quite extraordinary things like the 'Mad Minute'.[16] That army effectively ceased to exist by Spring 1915. The French Army, bled white by General Erich von Falkenhayn's forces around Verdun, was simply shattered as an offensive force by Summer 1916. Accepting the war on its own terms, the only Allied offensive option lay with green troops. The General Staff may have been both naive about the German defences, over-optimistic about the power of artillery and possessing inadequate communications. However, out of the appalling catastrophe of the Somme emerged a British Army tactically, if not strategically, ready to prosecute war. The Creeping Artillery Barrage began to be perfected, new technology (including tanks) was increasingly integrated into infantry tactics and, well, the conscript infantry began to have a clue. If Tommy Atkins needed his colleague beside him to stiffen his resolve, at platoon and company level he began to operate at speed and in confidence.

But that is not to deny that the story of the Somme, most especially its First Day, is one of disaster. By November, the British alone had lost over 400,000 casualties. It has been estimated that if they were to line up four a breast and march past the Cenotaph on Whitehall, then as the first four passed the final four would be lined up in Durham. The stories of the Pals Battalions are undoubtedly full of pathos.[17] They were not comprised of the innocent in any exceptional sense, of course. The Salford and Trafford Pals, for example, would have included some pretty hardened types, with all the toughness and bravado of people who had grown up around docklands. One only needs to read Robert Roberts' *The Classic Slum* to recognise these civilians turned soldiers would not have been naive soft-bellied fools. These were people used to the rough and tumble of city living and perhaps desperate to escape the depredations that came with that. One of the many things that life in the army offered the ragged and the poor was regular food and shelter and a sense of consistency in a capricious world. But the civilian army, raised on the back of Kitchener's Call, were, at a profound military level, innocents. The toughness of life in Edwardian slum Manchester and Salford cannot be over-stated. Here was the daily presence of the 'feeble-minded, dummies (deaf-mutes), hydrocephalics, grotesque cripples and its elderly women, broken like horses, who could be hired to drag a hundredweight of coke in a wagon a mile or more for threepence.'[18] Death was a constant companion. Indeed 'a recurrent event in the district was the death of some baby suffocated by its mother in bed.'[19]

Yet these children of the slums were as innocent as lambs in the face of what they met on the banks of the Somme and the Ancre in 1916. For, in a sense, who could not be? There were, of course, British soldiers present that summer who had experienced 1st Ypres or Loos, who had seen what industrial warfare could do, but perhaps not on the scale of what happened. For the First Day of the Somme had commenced after the greatest artillery bombardment seen until that time. Surely nothing could survive it – neither wire nor flesh. Yet the Germans had dug in during the quiet days from late 1914 to mid 1916 and they had dug in to stay. They waited in dug-outs, often fitted up with furniture and even pianos, up to thirty metres under the ground for the shells to stop. Crucially, the wire hadn't been cut. The Brits, despite the sheer volume of *matériel*, had too many shrapnel shells instead of high explosive. Shrapnel was devastating against flesh, but useless against wire. And the British had yet to perfect the trick of the Creeping Barrage or the quick-fire and support infantry tactics that the Germans put to such good use in the Spring Offensive of 1918. This was an age of innocence in more ways than one.

I was a little disappointed when I found out that Grandad Collins had – after being wounded on the Somme – been moved from the Worcestershire Regiment to the Labour Corps. Truth is that part of me – a part perhaps of all who secretly long for glory and who have yet to divest themselves of the myth of military honour – wanted something a little more glorious. At least Grandad Sam had been seconded – via the Worcestershire Yeomanry – to the Royal Dragoon Guards at one point. When I thought about the Labour Corps all I could call to mind was hapless Norman Wisdom in the film *The Square Peg* in which he and 'Mr Grimsdale' play low-grade pioneers caught up in Second World War shenanigans. All I thought of was road-mending and digging and carrying the stuff the actual fighting units needed. This was the place where the runts of the litter – like the little guy forever played by Wisdom – were sent.

While there will always be some truth in this picture of the pioneers – and Bert was never a big man or the brightest or most talented – the realities of the Great War changed this stereotyped picture. After September 1914 this was not a war of movement and élan. There were elite units that both the Germans and the British feared – that is, units always looking to be aggressive and take advantage. For the British and the French, eager to expel the occupier this was always a more highly prized virtue than the Germans (thus the often shameful state of allied trenches compared to the Germans). However, this – above all other wars – was a war in which men were done to rather than doing. This was a war where – until new tactics and technologies like the tank began to bite – was less about the infantry and more about artillery. The key fear of the war lay in what was falling from above. Indeed, soldiers quickly learned the reports of the various guns and mortars. The notorious Whizzbang was even immortalised in song. There must have been something singularly terrifying about

55

being a soldier – trained, in the very least, for attack and hand-to-hand combat – to find that the war's reality was helplessness.

Some theories of the emergence of so-called 'shell-shock' as a mass phenomenon in the war were based on the notion that trench warfare 'unmanned' or 'feminised' men – leaving them impotent to act, forever waiting on the impersonal shells that were the war's true agent.[20] 'One does not fight with men against *matériel*,' Petain, the French Great War commander said, 'It is with *matériel* served by men that one makes war.'[21] In this war, the relative status of units became less significant. The Labour Corps were as likely to be in the face of danger as the Irish Guards. Their skills and courage could rival that shown by the prestigious. Above all, that cream of the pre-war army, the Cavalry, discovered its emerging obsolescence.

Such is the nature of the Labour Corps that it merits little more than a footnote in the annals of military honours. I do not know if anyone from it made a great impact on the war or won a VC. It was not that kind of organisation. It was mostly made up of men who'd been smashed up badly by front-line action, who were no longer A1. My grandfather was not a VC type, if there is one. These were people more sinned against than sinning; more done to than doing. Four and half million men and women passed through the armed services in the Great War. The vast majority of them – like Bert and Sam – were ordinary nobodies. Some of them found a moment for glory or an opportunity for bravery under fire and received the Military Medal or suchlike. (For this was an age when enlisted men received, for the most part, different medals to the commissioned.) Most – again like my grandfathers – came through only with the universally supplied campaign medals, their names, ranks and serial numbers etched in the sides, and the physical and mental wounds of battle. Some were swallowed up by the war. This was the fate of so many Pals Battalions. Streets and professions and whole swathes of municipal life were wiped out in the space of a few hours on 1 July 1916. Slums and towns and villages – places where these men were more than names – would never be quite the same again.

I've always been intrigued by the fact that J.R.R. Tolkien served in the Lancashire Fusiliers, the same regiment that the Salford and Trafford Pals battalions were part of. I have no idea if he came across them. I suspect not (by the end of the war, the pre-war two battalion regiment had expanded to over twenty-four battalions). But, at a broader level, I like to think he remembered this civilian army, this military machine made up of little, ordinary folk rather than the great and the good, when he wrote his Middle Earth fantasies. Reading *The Lord of the Rings* is simultaneously like a journey across the front line and a lament for a socio-linguistic system that perhaps never was – a system which took glory and honour for granted, a world where good ultimately triumphs over evil. And the fact that, ultimately, the Ring of Power is destroyed, the King returns and so on, only confirms (in the context of our modern condition) the book's status as lament. Watching Peter Jackson's film adaptations confirms that Tolkien's vision of the Dead Marshes, filled with the floating dead of an ancient war, is essentially the poisoned waste of Ypres or the Somme; Hobbits' burrows and the journey through the mines of Moria are markers of the Great War's Troglodyte World; the mood of the novel is anxiety about the corrosive effect of industry on settled pastoral existence, echoes perhaps of the pre-war influence of William Morris and the Arts and Crafts movement. And the true heroes of the piece are, as troubled warrior Boromir describes them, 'the little ones' – the hobbits who are simple and courageous and trusting and bold; who are exceptional only in their basic goodness. Supreme among them is Frodo.

Frodo himself is an example of that key Great War archetype: the soldier whose wounds will never truly heal. Like my own grandad's leg wound that troubled him his whole life, Frodo's wound on Weathertop cannot be properly healed. At the end of the quest Frodo tells Samwise: 'I tried to save the Shire, and it has been saved, but not for me' and he leaves for the Grey Havens with the last of the Elves. Their going is the passing of an age. Frodo is the shell-shocked soldier, the wounded hero, the man whose nightmares won't fade and we journey with him every time we pick up the books or watch the films. The Great War remains with us in Tolkien's over-written pages, but it is how it is with us that intrigues me: as a kind of lament for a lost innocence, for identities before they were compromised and broken. If it is a badly written book, then what it writes most badly is the War, which is the story's true shadow.

Whenever I think of that wayside memorial on Trafford Grove and the others in dozens of other places I am shattered by the affection, pride and sadness the fact of their existence contains. Each name was a person before they became a name on a scroll. But I also sense such scrolls are not enough. For the 'little people' they commemorate warrant more. These are people, like my grandfathers, whose voices never carried very far. If they were anything like Grandad Collins, they were quiet dignified folk, whose own lack of voice and linguistic gifts mirrored the reality of their place in society. They were nobodies. Their true commemoration is the way we choose to live and the way we pass their stories down from parent to child, from aunt to nephew. This is a matter of politics and community in which the least are not to be mocked, but are honoured as sisters and brothers. The people on the Rolls of Honour were simple civilians caught up in terrific, terrible things. They are us and we are them. And we dare not ever forget it.

CHAPTER FOUR

'A Wallet' – Who and what was worthy of remembrance?

In Bertrand Tavernier's 1989 film *La vie et rien d'autre* there is a striking scene. It's 1920 and relatives of the French missing and dead of the war move along trestle tables covered with the possessions of the lost. In a field just behind the old front lines women and men search for the ring, the lighter or the diary that will give shape to their grief, that will tell them once and for all that they are widows or grieving parents. Perhaps for us the time has come for the intellectual turning over of the war's cultural artefacts to stop. We are too distant from the war. We are the children, grandchildren, perhaps great-grandchildren of the widowed, the bereaved and those who survived. Increasingly, we are people from all over the world who have no stake in the events of 1914–18 and care nothing for what it means. So, maybe it's time perhaps to stop troubling the missing of no-man's-land and allow their silence to speak.

In my hands is the brown leather wallet, made soft as ground chalk by use and love, that Grandad Sam carried with him across France and Palestine and later down the years as he became the twinkling man I learned to love. This is something made for a back pocket, to be opened expansively. Masculine as a shaving brush, it should be full of those huge old bank notes our ancestors used. For Sam it rarely was. It is not much of a keepsake. But it is what we, my family, have. As I hold it I think of that poem by Larkin, 'Mr Bleaney', a study of a dead man told via the character of the room he was finally reduced to. The closing lines are especially haunting: '...Telling himself that this was home...And at his age having no more to show/Than one hired box should make him pretty sure/ He warranted no better, I don't know.'[1]

It is, like much of Larkin's mature work, a study of the intimacy of loneliness and what remains after the impetus of hope has decayed. In the absence of a proper adult understanding of Grandad Sam, and the fact both that my own father is reticent about talking about him and we have few of his things – his wallet, a medal or two, some old photographs – I am drawn to read him through the categories of Bleaney: The settled (working-class) habits of a man gone to seed ('I know his habits – what time he came down,/his preference for sauce to gravy') who is ultimately left alone with little; the poverty of both the stories about him ('"Mr Bleaney took/My bit of garden properly in hand."') and the poverty of old age on a small pension ('"This was Mr Bleaney's room" ... Flowered curtains, thin and frayed,/Fall to within five inches of the sill'). The genius of Larkin is the space he gives for others to weave their own and their families' stories into his narratives of failure and loss. Whatever else might be said about Larkin, his brilliance lies in the restraint of his image and form. If his poems are, in the purest sense, inventions, they are also mythic, for they overlay the 1950s and 1960s with a pall of lost possibility, or cheap glamour ('The Whitsun Weddings') and smoky ennui ('Here'). Larkin both 'writes' my Grandad Sam (who, by the mid-1960s, was entering the final decade of his life) and 'writes' a nation weary from two world wars and the end of its global power.

I am trying to remember my grandfathers and honour them, but this wallet and what it evokes reminds me that, in some ways, it is a doomed task. I have too little information about them, especially Sam. My dad is his only child and he had a curious and complex relationship with him. As for my dad himself, he is quiet and self-reliant. There is no one else to tell Sam's story and he is relatively taciturn about Sam. It is a reminder of how quickly the living fall into myth and must be read through myth and symbol. We are so very distant from the war now. Our relatives have, like the original victims of the war explored in Tavernier's film, become nothing more than the artefacts we have of them. Of course men like Sam were forgotten almost from the moment the Great War ended. At one level, the evidence suggests that that is what they wanted. For though we are now inclined to view the war through the educated and war-troubled lenses of Sassoon, Owen and Graves and our rituals of remembrance seemed to have existed forever, the initial response to armistice was, arguably, 'Let's get on with our lives. Let us forget.'

The French poet Paul Valéry, writing in 1922, suggested that among the things injured by the war was the mind: 'The mind has indeed been cruelly wounded.... It doubts itself profoundly.'[2] With doubt comes flight: flight from reality, shaped around a desire for newness. The craving for newness in the 1920s was, in essence, a craving for new values. And, in saying this, I'm not simply buying into the 'dream of the Twenties' – the antics of sweet young things, of dandies and Dadaists, of Surrealists and Expressionists. This craving for newness, this crisis of value, became part of the mood of the post-Great War world affecting veteran and non-veteran, young and old, rich and poor. One expression of this lay in the formation of The League of Nations almost immediately after the war. People like Vera Brittain talk of the hunger for a new start on the part of both those who'd served and the young generation coming up.[3] Peace, they hoped, would not be a temporary cessation of violence until the next war, but a new way of going on. The League of Nations was to be the covenantal expression of that.[4]

Arguably, for much of the 1920s, the War was repressed as 'the Past': Veterans associations were not initially popular; ex-servicemen were not popular employees; the literary memoir texts by which we know the Great War did not saturate the market until the verge of the 1930s; Owen, the poet whom everyone knows, was not properly available until the 1930s. The 1920s were in so many ways a decade of repression. Modris Eksteins expresses it succinctly: 'As people became less able to answer the fundamental question of the meaning of life – and the war posed that question brutally in nine million cases – they insisted all the more stridently that the meaning lay in life itself, in the act of living, in the vitality of the moment.'[5] The senses and the instincts were indulged, and self-interest became, more than ever before, the motivation for behaviour.

This immediacy, this indulgence of instinct and desire, was not the preserve of an urban elite. The 1920s were an age of movement – of the proper emergence of flight (both as reality and metaphor), but also of improved train and bus services. Town and village were linked better than ever; and the local was exposed, through the phenomenon of cinema, to a vast world in undreamt of ways. The returning veterans took their expanded worlds back up the country lanes from which they had gone years before. The new and terrible was held, like a secret, in their itching, lice-filled clothes. And cinema exploded in all its fullness in this decade. The American word 'movie' captures all we need to know about this post-war era: it was an era of movement, where the flickering light of cinema captivated the attention of an audience for as long as it took for the next image to appear. Celebrity, the twinkle of stars on a silver screen, both brought audiences close to and distanced them from new worlds and people realised that there were new stars fixed in or falling through the firmament. To put things another way, the 1920s signalled, through the medium of the Great War, the triumph of art in daily life as understood by the pre-war avant-garde. Art triumphed over history, and the dominant mood of society was avant-garde. This was the triumph of spectacle and event not only in art, but also in life.[6]

Of course, to claim that 'art triumphed over history' is an appealing academic punt that constantly risks erasing the 'facts' of most people's lives. To claim that the likes of Granny and Grandad

Collins lived under conditions of the avant-garde borders on the comedic. Yet, they like most in the post-War era were inheritors of a world coming of age in new ways, especially through transport and cinema. However, I'm inclined to argue that my grandparents' experiences were erased in more obvious ways. When the memoirs of the war began to emerge in the late 1920s, when R.C. Sheriff's play *Journey's End* began stunning West End audiences and Owen's work became available for the first time, we should not pretend that it was the likes of Grandad Sam who were being recognised. The key voices 're-presenting' the War were the likes of Sassoon and Blunden and Graves. Their perspectives were those of the officer and privileged classes. Ford Madox Ford's work *Parade's End* is an extraordinary Modernist accomplishment, brilliant not least because it does not take the War as its subject, but places it in the context of the intrigues of class and power. But it is still a privileged voice. Vera Brittain's memoir *Testament of Youth* speaks from a woman's perspective, but its story centres on the golden children of privilege.

The subaltern voices of rural working-class men like my grandfathers were elided. They had not the words or money or access to publishers and education to write a memoir even if they'd wanted to. The working-class memoirs which did ultimately emerge tended to reflect an ingestion of the tropes of the privileged writers.[7] Crucially the way we remember and therefore memorialise the War is not via a working-class memoirist like Charles Bricknell, but the privileged voice of a Robert Graves. It was not until the Great War had reached the edge of human memory that many of the lower class voices began to be attended to.[8] It is only now that the Great War is pure history that stories like that of Ronald Skirth – the ordinary Tommy who became a pacifist while serving at the front and engaged in stunning acts of sabotage like altering the angles of guns so that shells would fall harmlessly – have properly come to be celebrated.[9] The War, one suspects, is something we always use to tell stories about ourselves. The time for prioritising the upper-middle class 'disillusioned' voice has past. Now we prefer voices that represent the ordinary and those who directly resisted the conflict.

But the elision of the likes of Sam from memory was perhaps more banal. Let me put it like this – when we think of the war, what images come instinctively into our minds? Beyond peradventure, it will be the trenches and barbed wire and the 'horror' of the static war. We shall be with Owen and Sassoon. We shall be with the Pals Battalions of Accrington and Salford and Sheffield. We shall think of those iconic photos of Ypres and Passchendaele. We shall be in hell. Few, if any of us, will think of the vast spaces and deserts of Mesopotamia. We shall not be in the bush of East Africa. Unless we are Australian or New Zealanders we are unlikely to think of the high cliffs and terrifying beachheads of Gallipoli. Some might imagine the derring-do of the knights of the air, of Von Richthofen and Brown. Almost no one will think of the grim encounter of dreadnoughts in the Jutland Sea. For the Great War *is* the Western Front for us.

Grandad Sam's war culminated in Palestine, Syria and Jordan as batman to Lord Hampton. There is a photo of him outside some barracks, sat high on his horse. To this untrained eye, he had a good seat and a nice straight back. The Middle East must have seemed like a sweltering, dusty dream to this man who'd spent his youth in the lush hills and fields of the Severn valley. The Middle Eastern campaigns have always been swathed in a cloak of mystery and romance, not least because of the mythologising of that curious rogue, meddler and hero, Colonel T.E. Lawrence. For perhaps Lawrence – who was his own greatest mythologiser – gave the imperial mind images more suited to its self-image than the squalid mud of Ypres. Lawrence was more of a creature out of a John Buchan or Erskine Childers' novel than the reality presented by soldiering on the Western Front. In the Desert, Lawrence and his kin were still playing 'The Great Game of Adventure and Empire', influencing 'the tribes' and making (and perhaps breaking) nations. Arguably the most abiding impact of the Great War was not on Western Europe, but on the fractures created in

Egypt, Iraq, Iran and Arabia by British and French imperialism. The post-war Paris Peace Conference re-wrote the map of the region. As the later Field Marshal Lord Wavell wrote in a letter at the time, 'After "the war to end war" they seem to have been pretty successful in Paris at making a "peace to end peace".' If the Europe we have today reflects the effects of the Great War – including the 1939–45 War – how much more so, the area commonly called the Middle East?

Here was a clash of empires – British and Ottoman – where (because of the apparent decline of the Ottoman Empire[10]) the British could still clearly present themselves as 'Top Dog'. And, perhaps as with a later war, the Desert itself was a supreme character in the romance of conflict, in its expression of old glories. For, as with the battle between the Desert Rats and the Afrika Korps in the Second World War, the Desert Campaign in the Great War offered greater scope for 'pure' battle between armies. As soldiers put it – in relation to the Western Desert in 1942 – the real enemy was the desert. Here were no churned up fields of France, sodden and stinking; here was a landscape that offered mirage and oasis. Here was the theatre for a great director like David Lean to make the 1962 movie, *Lawrence of Arabia*, a defining moment in how we see Lawrence and the Middle Eastern campaigns to this day: vast, impossible, shimmering and thrilling. Élan and dash – those great cavalry virtues – were not quite dead in Palestine and Mesopotamia in 1917.

Being a batman or 'soldier-servant' as it was then more properly known, could be a cushy number. Sam – who, rumour has it, always liked a bit of the easy life – would have welcomed the potentially better rations and the chance for a quick advancement. Being a batman meant you could get promoted reasonably quickly without any unnecessary heroism. Solder-servants were often lance-corporals, but could become sergeants, without the attendant company or platoon responsibilities. Sam ended the war a sergeant. The extra pennies would have been welcome, even if he was Hampton's dogsbody. Given that batmen were typically personally chosen, it might even have been an honour. For a simple country boy, being a Lord's *de facto* valet at the age of barely twenty was not to be sniffed at.

In Sam's world the feudal bonds had yet to be broken. To return to my previous discussion of Tolkien and the place of the War in *The Lord of the Rings*, the relationship between Samwise Gamgee and Frodo was based on Tolkien's experience of the batman/officer relationship. As Tolkien put it in a private letter, 'My Sam Gamgee is indeed a reflexion of the English soldier, of the privates and batmen I knew in the 1914 war, and recognised as so far superior to myself.' The batman/officer relationship was one of the last great expressions of the English Pastoral, celebrated later in the Peter Wimsey/Bunter relationship of Dorothy L. Sayers' novels. Sometimes – as in Sayers' mysteries – the bonds were strong enough that post-war the batman would become a regular servant of the officer. Indeed, as Sayers suggests in her classic series, the batman/officer relationship could be the basis – within the strict divisions of English class – for bonds of profound respect, affection and friendship. As Wimsey says to Bunter in *Whose Body*, 'I pay you £200 a year to keep your thoughts to yourself,' yet it is on Bunter whom Wimsey so often relies as partner in detection. Their relationship is grounded in their solidarity as survivors, in which Bunter movingly plays the father's role. When Peter has a recurrence of shell-shock, Bunter – as his former Sergeant – takes command of the situation. Affectionately, boldly and movingly assessing that Peter has been over-doing it, he says of his former Major, 'Bloody little fool.'

Despite our modern fascination with the upstairs/downstairs of country house life and the servant/master dynamic,[11] there is a profound sense in which this almost feudal, class-shaped reality has become unimaginable. Perhaps that is why we find the dynamic fascinating – because we feel safely distant from what it actually meant. It has become reduced to the safe glow of heritage. The 'country house' world of old bonds is – with a few exceptions – utterly dead. The Second World War killed it, even if it flickered in a few places for a few decades more. Even in Edwardian England, the numbers of domestic servants were dropping as other opportunities, especially for women, began to emerge. Things moved more slowly in the countryside. Grandad Sam and some of his family worked for large parts of their lives in service, in Sam's case for the Earl of Dudley at Witley Court. It was a world of poor pay, of sometimes unexpected opportunity (Aunty Betty, a lady's maid, spent part of every year in Monte Carlo and other glamorous places), of insecure contracts and where young women were especially vulnerable to the sexual advances of their 'masters'. The world imagined in Robert Altman's *Gosford Park* – especially the hierarchies of the servants' hall and the complex servant/master sexual relationships – is perhaps more accurate than we might expect.

Edwardian England was notoriously class-bound. The Great War could not kill that. But the sheer universality of death and the fact that more often than not junior officers and enlisted men were living cheek by jowl in filth or dust, sometimes for years at a time, flattened a stratified world. Front-line soldiers – enlisted and commissioned – shared a common bewilderment at staff plans which rapidly fell apart in the reality of conflict. Such was the level of attrition that, for the first time in British military history, experienced and skilled NCOs might rise to a (temporary) commission.[12] But despite the suspicion and snobbery and slights of class, on the front line at least, new relationships between the classes were forged. If post-war, most returned to their relative spheres, young men could not quite see each other the same again. The enlisted man saw that the greatest privilege accorded to the newly minted, Oxbridge, upper-middle class 2nd Lieutenant was a higher likelihood of rapid death. For the junior officer was expected to 'get out there', on patrol, to show 'dash' and all that. They were killed in disproportionate numbers, something reflected in the 'honour rolls' of the universities, post-war. Oxford's roll of honour contained 14,561 names, of which 2,680 were killed, died of wounds or sickness. Trinity, Cambridge, lost over 600 of its former undergraduates.[13]

Yet England had not seen anything like this immense civilian army before. The pre-war professional army had reflected the worst of the Victorian/Edwardian stratification of class. Officers needed to maintain a place in the Mess and, given the relatively small wages on offer, independent means were almost a given. The other ranks were drawn – as so often today – from among the poorest and most desperate. The civilian army of 1916 reflected all trades, professions and classes. A new world was emerging in which all classes suffered. Niall Ferguson offers a helpful corrective when he reminds us that, despite the myth of the lost generation being the brightest and best, the most privileged and the shining ones, such was the nature of the civilian army that it was the trades – the lower-middle classes and the working classes – who paid the greatest price.

Growing up in a Worcestershire village in the 1970s I witnessed the last of a feudal hierarchy whose death knell had been sounded in 1914. When I was born, the traditional 'squire' family were still in residence in the big house on the hill. The vicar and his wife still resided in the enormous Georgian rectory near the church. The great and the good of the village lived in the comfortable detached houses that gathered around the church. The grass tennis court of one was still tended by a gardener and the Bishop of Worcester – a personal friend of the Queen – held court in the Castle. When the Queen or her near relatives visited we'd be dragged out of the tiny Church of England school to wave our little flags. The ladies and gentlemen of the village would still head dutifully to church each Sunday, and organise fêtes and fairs. The kids learnt to dance the maypole and gave thanks to God for his bounty every Harvest.

The village was divided between the estate where we lived – the residences of the rural working class – and the main village where our betters lived. Yet when a new executive estate of detached new-builds was on the cards in the mid-1970s, poor and genteel were united in opposition. For the middle-classes were the common enemy. The incomers could not appreciate that in the country, the working class have always had more in common with the gentry than with the middle classes or even the urban working class. Our pastimes – country sports, love of horses and the open spaces – are shared. Rural life, for rich or poor, has never been especially cultured.

By the end of the 1970s, Grandad Sam was dead, along with many of the cultural 'markers' he'd grown up with. By modern standards, Sam was still a relatively young man when he died in 1975, but he had become an old man and his world was coming to a close. In our village, by the late 1970s, the manor-house family had moved out of the big house on the hill into a more manageable, smaller modern place. Their home ultimately was taken over by 'trade' – a businessman from Birmingham. The great rectory had become too costly to heat and fell into disrepair. The church now owns a modest four-bedroom place that hasn't been used properly for ten years, since the vicar now lives in another village of his increasingly extended patch. And still a few of the respectable families show their faces in church, but it is not like it was. Because they know that duty no longer requires it. The old need to demonstrate one's respectability has gone. And perhaps their station in life has diminished too. The Bishop no longer lives in the Castle, but a more functional residence in Worcester. The world has moved on for both the traditional rural working and gentry classes.

In his famous poem, 'A Worker Reads History', Bertolt Brecht seeks to remind the reader who the true agents of history are. 'Who built the seven gates of Thebes?/The books are filled with names of kings./Was it the kings who hauled the craggy blocks of stone?...And even in Atlantis of the legend/The night the seas rushed in,/The drowning men still bellowed for their slaves./Young Alexander conquered India./He alone?' Brecht is not speaking out of a rural, feudal voice of stratified ties, but an urban Socialist one. I don't think working-class rural folk like my grandparents (or even my parents) would much care for Brecht's barely concealed anger about who makes history and who gets forgotten in the process. They were raised to serve and – the important grace of being permitted to grumble aside – to accept their lot. But there are days when I can barely contain my fury at the layers of silence imposed on Sam and Bert, and on their wives May and Doll, by the myth of England and its tales of hope and glory. For if there has been a concerted attempt to recover the forgotten voices of the Great War – among the ordinary as well as the great – the likes of Sam and Bert have always been assigned a role among the support cast. Perhaps they did not do remarkable things. Unlike Lord Hampton, the man Sam served in war, my grandfathers didn't get to lead organisations and do not warrant a place in the National Archives. Maybe they wouldn't want that anyway. But they, because of accidents of birth and the structures of their world, did not get a chance. Each page of history may be cast a victory, but as Brecht asks, 'At whose expense the victory ball?'

A friend recently told me about a visit – a pilgrimage – she made to her childhood town, a place she left for university nearly thirty years ago. She and her sister visited her old school – a secondary modern that had been converted into a comprehensive in the 1960s. It was a good place to go to school, she thought, in which opportunities had been given to her and others, irrespective of class, to get on and not be afraid to try. But when she visited the old place it had been flattened, to be replaced by a new-build out of town, all contemporary curves and Scandinavian pine finish. And, as far as she knows, nothing was taken from the old building to be incorporated into the new. By contrast, she visited the private school down the road – an old school, of fine stone and solidity and care, a building that has been preserved and augmented over time. And her thought was this: 'My past was not worth preserving.' Some stories seem to count more than others. We might argue over the extent to which this is justified or true. That some stories seem to count more, are worthy of honour or preservation, simply because of accidents of birth, privilege, money or power is not to be borne. Yet this so often seems to be how our economy of remembrance works.

Of course, it is never simple. I may be an urbanite, a socialist and all the rest. I may see how my family – because of accidents of birth and so on – have been cast as the servants of undeserved privilege. But there is enough of the rural working class child in me that part of me laments an England now lost. Reason and sense tells me that the England of my grandparents and parents, the England into which I was born was an unfair, prejudiced and exploitative place. It had been built on dubious foundations through the commercial exploitation of the world. And yet it was an England in which there was still pride, in which patriotism didn't necessarily mean xenophobia and which meant that servant and officer class might face impossible situations in the worst war ever known and somehow not break. This was my grandparents' world and so I cannot quite disown it. I see the bullshit and the lies which this myth conceals and also depends upon, yet it is part of me too. It has shaped me and so I cannot quite let the story die. Myths make and shape us.

Larkin, that most English poet, understood the myths we use to trick, make and live our selves. Even in this most individualistic of times, it is community that shapes – family, church, civic or national. England was never quite as he described it in his Great War poem, 'MCMXIV', and yet his pictures haunt us still. His images of the men lined up to enlist have a cinematic clarity and verity ('The crowns of hats, the sun/On moustached archaic faces/ Grinning as if it were all/An August Bank Holiday lark') while the repeated use of the subjunctive 'as if' creates both a sense of stasis and unreality. This is a world fixed in aspic – a world of 'farthings and sovereigns,/And dark-clothed children at play/Called after kings and queens.' It builds to its horrifyingly simple conclusion: 'Never such innocence,/Never before or since,/As changed itself to past/Without a word … Never such innocence again.'

No one should believe the myth of Edwardian innocence. The pre-Great War world was hardly the Kingdom of Heaven. The experiences of many people in Ireland, India, Southern Africa 'testify to that. So, too, the experiences of the working classes in England, without access to comprehensive health and welfare systems. Yet, because the Great War signalled the end of Britain's supreme, unquestioned place at the 'Top Table of the World', it is inevitable that those of us who are inheritors of that 'Fall from Place' risk being mesmerised by that era and, at a human level, by our families' role within it. I am so very glad that the UK has changed and become something new – multi-ethnic, inter-cultural, committed to a health service free at the point of need and so on. In a time when many use the myth of England's or Britain's 'greatness' for xenophobic and isolationist ends, the vision of a complex, diverse nation has never been more urgent. In our 'post-Brexit' world the need to see 'Britain' clearly has never been greater. I despair at politicians and senior military staff desperate to pretend that we are still a world power and who chase after the crumbs offered by the American top table. But we cannot also hide from our myths and our past even if we try to lay them down. 'England' – because of what happened to her in 1914 and what we might have become without that cataclysm – haunts us and perhaps always will.

CHAPTER FIVE

'A Photograph' – 'Oh! What a feminist war'?

My family is hardly awash with photos of pre-1939 life. They were not of the kind of class who gathered large numbers of photos. Photos were for very special occasions, usually posed and still. Mine was a family who had yet to learn how to look at a lens or how a lens might look at them. Of the small number of old photos in my family 'archive' I have come to be haunted by one. It is not the image of Grandad Collins looking about twelve in a crude army cap, nor the strange sepia shots of Sam in the desert. It is a puzzling, mysterious portrait of my Aunty Betty looking directly into the camera. There is no date on it, but given the style of her hair and age it must have been taken in the early 1920s at the latest. She looks no older than twenty-five and, to my generous eyes, she is rather beautiful, the left side of her face slightly in shadow and rather more open than the right, the merest hint of a smile on her face. I do not know if this 'face on the edge of a smile' is some conscious echo of the Mona Lisa or was fashionable at the time, but its curious power over me lies in its ambiguity. There may be a hint of a smile, signalling the reticence of her Edwardian generation, but there is also something unutterably sad in that look. The beauty somehow lies in the brokenness.

It is very easy to focus – as I have done – on the men of the Great War. Such were the levels of the slaughter, almost exclusively focused (in Britain's case at least) on male members of the armed forces that it is almost unavoidable. Though there were raids on England – primarily the Zeppelin threat – and, close to the front lines, nurses were killed, the Great War was very different to the Second World War. The differences between the front and 'Blighty' were sometimes shattering. Many of the memoirists draw attention to the 'deficit' between the realities of the front and the 'unrealities', as they saw it, of Home. But from a woman's point of view the war was simultaneously marked by extraordinary new possibilities outside the home, the hope of new things to come – not least suffrage – and, of course, the expectation of pain and loss. If working-class women had always worked, for the first time, relatively large numbers of women began to discover their earning power. They were not to be read as mothers or wives or servants or, indeed, as secondary. Women became essential to the national struggle and economy. Women worked on the land, in factories and undertook extraordinarily dangerous work like shell-making. If this liberation into the independence of earning a wage for oneself was (for some at least) temporary, it set a precedent for change.

Equally, the Great War was a time of waiting and promise. The Women's Suffrage movement had been involved in the most committed, vigorous campaign to gain votes for women. Under the influence of Emmeline and Sylvia Pankhurst, the war signalled an end to much of the direct action associated with the movement; lobbying continued, but quietly and, as Loch Mowat puts it, 'what Mrs Pankhurst and the suffragettes had battled for in vain was conceded in wartime with hardly a flutter by the same Parliament which had so sternly refused it in peace.'[1] By the time of the so-called 'Coupon Election' of December 1918, six million women had been enfranchised.[2] During hostilities, women demonstrated their worth beyond the home, on the home front and in the casualty clearing station. But if this was a time of possibility it was, of course, still a time of pain. Women were still mothers, sisters, wives and lovers. Sons and fathers and brothers and sweethearts were consumed by the war machine.

I only knew my Aunty Betty as a rather small, delicate old woman with a love of cigarettes. I cannot think of a situation where she didn't have one clamped in her mouth or between her nicotine-stained fingers. She died when I was nine. In some ways she made no great impression on me. This was hardly surprising given that she lived with her sister, the imperious Aunty Chris, who, it was clear to me, even as a child, was one hell of a terrifying woman (part Margaret Thatcher, part Duchess of Devonshire). She had kept an hotel with her husband and was one of the lady members who kept the Worcestershire county cricketers and members fed. It was through Betty that I came to understand the notion of 'maiden aunt', for she had never married. Indeed, the story in my family is that she had only ever had one sweetheart and he had been killed in the war. It is perhaps too easy to read the effects of loss and loneliness into that curious photo of Betty. It is easy to assume that she remained unmarried, in an age when the default position for women was marriage, because she never quite recovered from the loss of her lover. Like others in our family she went 'into service'. However, unlike much of my family her world was rather larger.

Betty was lady's maid to a grand woman who lived on Duke Street, Mayfair and got to see some of the more glamorous parts of the world with her. The only remaining evidence we have are a few letters from the 1930s, when it seems Betty had to take temporary leave and go and nurse either her mum or dad. They are striking for both their formality and affection. The 'mistress' writes of how Betty must ask for money if she needs it. Yet the formality is curious. Betty is referred to as 'Dear Mann' (keeping to the conventions of the day) and the lady refers to herself as 'Your affectionate mistress.' For a simple, uneducated country girl she got to enjoy more of the bright lights of the city than might have been her lot. Her collections of signatures and photos of the stars of stage and silver screen offer testimony to that. Yet, for me, she is a symbol of the abiding effects of the war. Though she was 'only' a servant, she was learning to act, to break free from the old ways. For me she represents the loneliness and opportunities that arise in the midst of loss. She is a symbol of the way the Great War created space for women to act.

Virginia Nicholson's book *Singled Out* is a meditation on the phenomenon of what came to be known as 'The Surplus Women' – the two million or so women who outnumbered men after the Great War. She provides extensive details of society hostesses exposed – post-Somme – to the poignant absences of eligible young men from their balls, dances and social events. Much as some may mock and question the world of privilege and power these images conjure, they remain powerful visions of a world that had been wiped out by the war, a world where the great expectation and right of women was to marry, have children and be accompanied through life. Nicholson also explores the story of Rose Harrison, maid to Nancy, Lady Astor. Harrison wrote one of the rare accounts of life as a lady's maid. In my mind, Harrison writes the story of my Aunty Betty and of large numbers of working-class girls around the time of the Great War.

Harrison indicates how marriage was the goal of every woman servant, yet aspects of the servant's life – even in the best of times – acted against it. 'After the war men were scarce, the demand far outweighing the supply and a maid's limited and irregular time off was an added disadvantage ... there was no status in being a servant, you were a nobody; marriage was the way out of it.'[3] Servants might expect an afternoon or evening off a week. Their lives were tied to houses or to the caprices of their employers. Their employment rights were among the worst in an already unfair society. The young women in service nonetheless would take whatever opportunity they could to have a good time and, ideally, find a man. Harrison tells a story of how – early in her career, serving Lady Tufton – the family and staff decamped from London to Westmorland every Christmas, where the female staff would compete with the local girls for the available male talent. The London girls were seen as sophisticates – as city slickers – and parlour maids and housemaids would descend *en masse* upon local dances to turn the eyes of the village boys. Gladys, the second parlour maid, achieved a big coup by snaring the Mayor of Appleby's son.

But if Harrison was admirably honest about the prospects for young women in this dying world of servants, of formal attire and of rigid relations between the classes, she was clear-eyed about her own ambitions. For, yes, she fancied men and for a while was engaged to be married, but at the same time, she wanted to 'get on'. Perhaps in our age, an age when women (in the countries of the Economic North at least) have increasingly taken up the most demanding political, scientific and managerial roles, we may be inclined to sneer at the narrow visions of work advancement available to lower-class, poorly educated girls like Rose and my Aunty Betty. But if a woman was prepared for the loneliness of being unattached and the opportunities which came for a talented singleton, she might – within reason – change her stars. Harrison recognised that her chance lay – like my Aunty Betty – as a lady's maid to a rich, cosmopolitan and influential woman. As Nicholson, concludes, 'Rose had set her heart on securing such a position and marriage just wasn't compatible with the hard work and long hours required of a personal maid.'[4]

Harrison served Lady Astor for thirty-five years. 'With Lady Astor she travelled the world, met the cream of international high society, and made herself indispensable to the doyenne of one of the first families in the land. Lady Astor's life was her life, eighteen hours a day, seven days a week; she had none of her own. That was the deal.'[5] As one of the servants in the film *Gosford Park* comments, in relation to the lady's maid of a baroness, 'Look at poor old Lewis, if her own mother had a heart attack she'd think it was less important than one of Lady Sylvia's farts.' This was the life of a lady's maid like my Aunty Betty. Yet, as her own life drew to its close, Harrison could write, 'The family were still there and have been to this day. "You will never want for anything, Rose," her ladyship often said to me. The children have seen to it that their mother's word has been honoured ... there is something else they have given me which has made my retirement the richer: their continued affection and interest. I visit them, they visit me. I am still one of the tribe."[6]

I am not a romantic about an era in which ambition for an Aunty Betty or a Rose Harrison meant effectively losing themselves to the whims of the privileged. As a feminist, one can hardly do anything but rejoice over the collapse of a social system which left not only poor girls like Betty or Rose, but middle-class and upper-class women with stark choices. In the vast majority of cases women's lives were shaped around patriarchal definitions of their lives. Marriage was one kind of ambition, but it signified a loss of independence and self-determination. For a lower-class girl it might mean a rubbish house, endless kids, and a life with no comforts and dependency. Singleness became, especially post-Great War, a means of channelling the limited opportunities of the day into the character of a rewarding life.

Yet if this era produced remarkable examples of self-willed and self-directed women – including the novelist Winifred Holtby, engineer Victoria Drummond and theatre impresario Rowena Cade – to see Betty's story as 'ambitious' or self-directed is dissonant. She seems only to have exchanged one form of self-abnegation – marriage – for another one at the hands of a wealthy patron. In our time of expanding and expansive opportunities for girls and women it is easy to dismiss Rose or Betty. But we should not. For if there have always been exceptional people who almost seem to treat social disadvantage as the axis around which they will break free of their limited world, most of us engage in humbler negotiations. We push at the edges of the possibilities, discovering opportunities, but also accepting huge aspects of our situation.[7] The likes of Betty or Rose had few advantages – no money and no education. It is a token of the appalling class and patriarchal divisions of the early twentieth century that opportunity might come in the shape of serving a spoilt aristocrat for eighteen hours a day. Future generations may yet find it absurd and bewildering that, as late as the early twenty-first century, women priests in the Church of England like me – for the most part – lived with circumstances that did not allow them to rise to the most senior roles within their organisation. We take the opportunities we can while both pushing for new horizons and living with injustice as a daily reality.

The poignant shadow across the life of my Aunty Betty was the death of her man in the Great War. My family do not even know who he was now. There is a photo of them together and that is it. He is, for us at least, utterly lost. His photo, in which we see him looking lovingly at Betty, makes it possible to see him, but only underlines his erasure. He has been reduced to paper. Yet, if I refuse to be romantic about the social injustices of the world Betty moved in, I struggle to be as cynical about matters of the heart. And, yes, the movement of time and the fact that we have little more than a single photograph of her and her chap together means pathos almost inevitably accrues to what might have a quite different reality. Just as I almost cannot help but read Betty's loss in that mysterious photo of her I love, I cannot but be moved by that other photo of her with her beau, standing in an orchard. Yes, the cynic in me knows that even if he'd survived the war, Betty's future with him would almost certainly have been no sunlit upland and would have held the prospect of drudgery within it; but the romantic believes it also promised companionship and the possibility of children.

Virginia Nicholson's book on the 'Surplus Women' contains powerful testimony to the way the lack of suitable husbands meant that huge numbers of women forewent the possibility of children – something that would have been seen as foundational for female identity. For someone like me, who – under other circumstances – has forgone children, I cannot help but be moved by this. Equally as someone who has sought to discern the shape of vocation and service in my own life, if in a different sphere, I am – to my surprise

– full of admiration for Betty's ultimate faithfulness to the woman she served. Service perhaps is not such a dirty word.

It is uncomfortable to think that as well as being a cultural, human and social catastrophe, the Great War may have provided unexpected opportunities, that it was the condition of change. But a catastrophe is precisely 'an overturning'. Only an ethically and emotionally undeveloped individual or community could will something on the scale of the Great War in order to accelerate social change.[8] The events on the Western Front have tended to glaze the pre-war era in aspic, as if without the disruption, Edwardian England and its settled inequalities might have continued unchallenged forever. To see the pre-war era as such is not least among the effects of the conflict, for Britain and the Empire were less settled than we often imagine. The abiding disruptions and challenges of British life in the decades before the war included the questions of Irish Home Rule and the status of women in society. Equally, working men and the Labour Movement were constantly challenging the hegemony of privilege. This was no static, comfortable land of hope and glory. Life in the decade and a half preceding 1914 has come to be viewed inevitably through the optic of the war that shattered it. Paul Fussell suggests, 'For the modern imagination that last summer [of 1914] has assumed the status of a permanent symbol for anything innocently but irrecoverably lost. Transferred meanings of "our summer of 1914" retain the irony of the original, for the change from felicity to despair, pastoral to anti-pastoral, is melodramatically unexpected.'[9] The struggles of Suffragettes, class unrest, Ireland on the brink of civil war are shaded and softened 'by the long, elegiac shadows cast by the war.'[10]

I'm not the first or last to be haunted by an old photograph. Sepia photos have a slightly ghosted quality, the result of the long exposure times. The ghosting gathers mystery to the images. Historical fashion and culture only add to their curious power. For – unlike today – the Victorian and Edwardian ages were constructing the language of visual representation. Long exposures may have required a kind of stillness on the part of subjects, but equally this was no age for gurning self-indulgence. Fashion dictated dignity, for photographs were – unlike today – not seen as throwaway. They were records for the ages. Centuries of portrait painting fashion – the preserve of the wealthy and important – was filtered into portrait photography. For the first time the relatively humble could lay down a record for the future. The lower classes could visually project virtues of dignity and solidity. And – as Raphael Samuel argues[11] – the posed family portrait is also a record of how the subject sees themselves and wants to be seen. The large Victorian family with its paterfamilias is a projection of patriarchal surety, propriety and civic munificence; the cool, still image of the officer about to head for the front is a statement of his attempt to project martial virtues of trustworthiness and unflappable solidity; the image of Betty is a projection of wistful longing and mysterious allure. Like the long traditions of Western art, it inevitably buys into a visual aesthetic that treats woman as objects of the male gaze. Yet, there remains to my eye at least, something wilful too. Betty is not merely being observed. The mystery lies in what she is trying to keep for herself. It is her defiance against what has been done to her and her generation.

Being creatures limited by time, it is unsurprising that we are haunted by the past – one's own and of one's community. Time ensures that living well entails loss. And so old photographs can haunt us in another way, for they remind us of our losses and mortality and fragility. Their power is such that one does not even need to know the person in the photo. The stillness, the ghosting and, of course, the sometimes obvious context helps. Thus, the potency of late Edwardian and Great War photography. Because of the events of 1914–18 we cannot help but read certain things into the last photo of the newly commissioned lieutenant in his awkward new uniform. We cannot avoid seeing innocence and naivety in the wispy smiles of young women in crisp white dresses posing on a lawn in 1912. We read our own losses and the losses of our culture and nation into them. The photos matter – redolent as they are of mystery, loss, and a certain sort of British reserve

– because they are records of absence. They are records of those who have disappeared. Above all, it is almost impossible not to be haunted by those sepia photos of the 1914 recruits: patient men, who could be waiting to enter a football match or a game of cricket. As Geoff Dyer strikingly suggests, 'the photographs of men queuing up to enlist seem wounded by the experience that is still to come: they are *tinted* by the trenches, by Flanders mud. The recruits of 1914 have the look of ghosts. They are queuing up to be slaughtered: they are already dead.'[12] Grandad Bert never lost that look.

I have a further, very personal reason why I am haunted by old photographs, whether of my family or of a more generic nature. And it is that I know only too well what it is to disappear from the record. So many of the photos that exist of me are records of absence in a quite particular way. There are a lot of photos of me, from my childhood and teens, which have effectively disappeared for they are never shown. For they tell the story of someone who is no longer here. They are a record of a young man who, as I've suggested in another book, I killed.[13] They are the photos which, when I changed sex in my early twenties, my parents and family filed away, perhaps never to be seen again. I own two photos of my male self: one of a five-year-old boy in a white sweater and blue shorts staring cheekily at the camera for his school photo and one passport photo, a dreadlocked, hirsute, smart-arsed twenty-one year old desperate to keep the world out. They are never taken out. They – like so many pictures of me – have been buried. They are dead bodies slowly turning into skeletons. The photos – a record of a deeply unhappy person – reveal and conceal, like almost every human artefact, in equal measure.

It has become almost unavoidable to read the Great War through anything other than literary categories. Paul Fussell went so far as to designate it, 'Oh what a literary war!' No other war has been written about in quite the same way. No other war feels quite so much like it has been written. Elegy has become the key mode of writing about the war and, in many ways, this book is beholden to that genre. But my search for Betty has a different character. I have pursued her with the energy of a romance. I have sought her out. In our crude, sexualised age this might seem odd. But the categories of romance do not seem inappropriate to me here – for, through the picture I love of her, I have been mesmerised. She dazzles me.

In classical and medieval romance, one of the clichéd, standard narratives involves a hero seeking to save a lady from an imperilling monster. The 'monster' which seems to imperil Betty and the women like her is the threat of their final and utter disappearance from memory and the public record. I sense our male heroes and relatives of the war generation are part of our cultural memory still, just about. Our interest in that era is guided by them. For as long as the Great War is spoken about, we shall return again and again to the front line, to no-man's land and the boys who went 'Over The Top'. Yet, if it would be easy to imagine myself as 'the hero' who is trying to save Betty from disappearance, the truth is that 'the work' flows the other way. She, along with her early twentieth century sisters, is the hero who helps save people like me from forgetting the stories of which we are part. Who shows us that without the spirit, love and defiance of our sisters – even the seemingly insignificant ones – we travel nowhere. They, as much as the Pankhursts and the Holtbys – were ground-breakers for the women we've become.

CHAPTER SIX

'A Church Cross' – How Great War cemeteries and memorials constructed memory and remembrance

It is almost too banal to acknowledge, but symbols are unavoidable. Anything, in principle, can become a symbol. Our capacity to make symbols is a mark of our creative humanity and capacity for community. They surround us and are within us, and they are both arbitrary and essential. Each Sunday I, like thousands of other priests, take bread and break it in community with others. We take wine, pour it, bless it and share it together. They are just bread and wine and yet they are not. They are the Body and Blood of Jesus Christ. Theologians have argued for centuries about the precise status of the blessed bread and wine. What is clear is that within the community of faith something extraordinary happens. Indeed, if in many circles, the priest has been seen to hold a special power or magic of transformation (summarised in the focus, for some, on the words of institution or, for others, the epiclesis[1]), the talk now is of the priest as 'presider' – that is, the one who presides over the prayer and work of the whole people. The Eucharist is a gathering up of what makes the Christian community the community of faith; and it is for the community of faith that the bread and wine become effective signs of Christ. Bread and wine are potent signs of the divine. They enable imaginations to participate in how we are fed by the Lord's broken body, or explore the notion of the sacrifice of blood as atonement and so on. Yet, arguably, this is a contingent matter.

The Cross has become a, if not the, key symbol of Christ and Christianity. This wasn't always so. The early church, for whom the Imperial means of torture was a present reality and which was always under threat of persecution, made use of other signs as well, including the famous fish symbol. Two centuries later, mosaics and church art indicate a fascination with shepherd images. There is evidence that the cross was associated with Christians certainly from the second century CE, for some of the early Church Fathers saw fit to defend themselves from accusations of worshipping a cross. However, the emergent dominance of the Cross as fundamental symbol of Christianity took time and represents the extent to which it is arbitrary. Yes, the Cross has not simply been plucked out of thin air – it is part of the received narrative about Jesus and his life. His death by an instrument of torture is – if one is asserting that he is saviour and king – striking and unexpected. Yet, there is no reason why the cross had to become the fundamental symbol of faith. To this day, in the Ethiopian Orthodox Church the key image of faith is the Madonna and Child.

At the end of the Great War there was extensive discussion about the symbols of death and remembrance. As the Menin Gate, that vast arch memorial to the missing of Flanders, signals for all to see, almost countless thousands of men were effectively vaporised by the war. They simply disappeared. Shells were so powerful that flesh and bone effectively ceased to exist. There was nothing left to bury.[2] Added to this was simple problem that early army-issue 'dog tags' – designed to ensure the identification of the lost – were made from leather and rapidly decayed. No one anticipated that some bodies would lie in no-man's-land, inaccessible to burial parties, for years at a time. For those who could be identified or had not simply been swallowed by shell holes and mud, attempts were made to provide burial. In 'hot' and fluid sectors this would at best be hasty. It might be in a mass grave. But markers – even if they were rapidly obliterated in a counter-attack or the next advance – had to be found. Inevitably soldiers, officers and chaplains reached for the symbols they knew best. Crude crosses – sometimes made of two bits of duckboard – sprung up all over France and Flanders. A cross was both easily improvised and, in a churned landscape, reasonably distinctive. Yet, given the cultural Christianity of the majority of combatants, the cross was always going to be the symbol of choice. The family of Jewish poet Isaac Rosenberg feared that he had been laid to rest under a cross. Quite apart from anxieties that Jewish, Muslim or Hindu and Sikh soldiers had been buried under the sign of Christianity, it was clear that the temporary, easily eroded symbols and markers of war could not do the work of the peace.

There was to be no repatriation of bodies. It was neither the Army's way nor was there any genuine logistical prospect that three quarters of a million British dead (and another quarter of a million Empire/Commonwealth dead) could be brought 'home'. The government listened to individual pleas for the return of loved ones – and endured an impassioned debate in parliament in 1920 – and decided that the fallen would remain where they lay. In relation to this point, Modris Eksteins relates one of those poignant, terrible ironies of the early moments of the war: On 19 December 1914, the 1ˢᵗ Rifle Brigade and the 1ˢᵗ Somerset Light Infantry attacked in mid-afternoon in broad daylight. An artillery barrage was supposed to have cut the wire, but just in case it hadn't each man was issued with a straw mattress to lay over the wire. As Eksteins suggests, 'The Germans must have been astonished by the bizarre sight that confronted them as the attack began.'[3] The wire wasn't cut, the soldiers were burdened not only by the mattresses, but also by all their sixty pounds of kit. They were cut down and fell with all their soldierly possessions, their soldierly identity and their mattresses, until no-man's-land resembled a bloody, muddy and perverse place of rest.

One of the most startling facts of the topography of the War is how one can be travelling through the region of the Somme and Ancre and have no sense that a war ever took place there and, then, suddenly be confronted with a series of small cemeteries located in the middle of fields. It is possible to follow the line of the First Day of the Somme battlefield by simply looking from cemetery to cemetery. Tragedy became a matter of geography. While there are many 'concentration' cemeteries in France and Belgium – where after the war the dead were collected together – on certain sections of the Line one can simply see, unfolding to this day, the principle that where a soldier fell, he was buried.

The debate over the nature of the headstones for the fallen reflected the significance of and the anxiety around symbols. The cross was for many in Georgian England, as now, the default, go-to symbol for death. Yet the Imperial War Graves Commission was charged with the unprecedented task of finding a way to commemorate all who had died in such a way that two things could be signified: the brotherhood of the battlefield and (despite the crippling class distinctions of the time) the equality of death and sacrifice. Britain was not the spectacularly inter- and multi-cultural nation it now is, but it was still a world empire. Not all who died under its flag were – within the conventional terms of the day – Christians. The cross was not a symbol for all. Ultimately the Commission settled on a simple headstone of Portland stone. Religious symbols and text could be added. Cemeteries with more than forty graves would typically add a Cross of Remembrance, designed by Reginald Blomfield – a Latin cross with the addition of a sword within its bounds, examples of which can be found not only in Europe, but in the UK and around the world. It has become a conservative classic of remembrance – the cross signifying the faith of the majority of those who died, the sword the martial context of its creation.

The Cross of Remembrance is also a salutary reminder of the tension found within Christianity. Sue Mansfield reminds us that one of the beloved images of traditional Christian art is the 'Harrowing of Hell'. In it, Christ is depicted emerging from hell, holding his cross as if it were a sword, leading the liberated patriarchs by the hand as if they were children. She concludes, 'In that one scene are caught the ambiguities toward war that have plagued Christianity from its beginning and made the civilisation founded upon it both more pacifistic in intent and more profoundly violent in action than any other culture that has existed. The ambiguity lies in the question of whether one sees the cross (the acceptance of suffering) as replacing the sword as a means of dealing with chaos and sin, or whether one sees it as simply a new and more effective sword with which to destroy the forces of evil.'[4]

In my home village, as in thousands of others, the absent dead still needed to be commemorated. Grief – perhaps made more acute by the absence of a body to bury or cremate – demanded it. The choice in my village was for a cross under which the names of the fallen could be inscribed. It was not grand or of limestone like Blomfield's proud imperial statement. It was of the local material – sandstone – and if it has presence/size it is because it is raised up in the graveyard. It does not have a sword etched into its cross. Significantly it is placed at the entrance to the church, as if to announce that remembrance of the Lost of the Great War is the very entry point into this village's rituals of death and memory. For if the baptismal font is traditionally placed at the entrance to the church itself, signifying the priority of that ritual as an entry into the life and death of Christ, so the Memorial Cross waits for us at the entrance point of the community's place of the dead. It is a guard and warning and call to pay attention to what this community considers significant.

As I've indicated elsewhere in this book, by the early twentieth century, the English rituals of death and remembrance were increasingly moving on from the traditional desire to be buried in the churchyard. The Imperial (later Commonwealth) Graves Commission's picture of the orderly graveyard away from that historical marker of faith, the church, was part of an emerging picture of death set in chain by the growth of municipal cemeteries in the nineteenth century. The mood of those cemeteries was fundamentally of rest: of freedom to ponder mortality liberated from images of the traditional ultimate judgment associated with the Church. In the military cemeteries around the Ancre, Somme and Ypres, the neat rows of graves in uniform Portland stone took the mood of rest and reflection to its ultimate conclusion. And how could one argue? All those who had lived and died in the chaos of a war without limit were to be offered the peace and order of kindly tended graves. In life they had been violated. In death they were to have dignity.

Geoff Dyer argues, 'In some ways the military cemeteries of the Great War represent the culmination and systematic application of developments in *civilian* cemetery design.'[5] They signify a shift in attitudes to death that had been gathering force since at least the Enlightenment. In short, as George Mosse summarises, 'The image of the grim reaper was replaced by the image of death as eternal sleep.'[6] As questions about public health became more prominent in the nineteenth century, civilian cemeteries were moved out to calm, shaded settings conducive to rest. 'Setting and symbolism encouraged a mood of pantheistic reflection rather than penitence and fear.'[7] As Bob Bushaway concludes, 'Not the construction of homes fit for heroes in post-war Britain, but the construction of vast cities of the dead, was to preoccupy the attention of British society throughout the period before the Second World War.'[8]

A contrast between British concepts of war cemeteries and those of the German and French is instructive. It's hardly surprising that the way the small number of German graveyards produce and perform memory is rather different to the British. Until 1954 there had been a wider number of German cemeteries in Belgium. However, for various reasons it was agreed to concentrate the German war dead of Belgian Flanders in three. Of these I've visited the most famous, Langemark. Langemark is an austere and ultimately bleak place. In some respects, it represents solemnity shorn of the last trace of sentiment. Love is not the central theme at

Langemark. The choice of materials for remembrance themselves have a grim seriousness. If the English and Commonwealth graves are instantly recognisable because of the Portland stone, the German ones have a different uniformity. Individual and collected graves (with up to ten bodies) are marked with small flat grave markers of granite. There is also a mass grave of nearly twenty-five thousand bodies contained in an area a few metres square. In one section lies the remains of a concrete bunker.

The profound sombreness of this place, with large oaks (Germany's national tree) growing into a large canopy around the site, has the character of the twentieth century's other world war. It is a chastening place. It is not a place to linger as conceivably one might in one of the small British graveyards. It produces a troubled remembrance, not gratitude. This, of course, may reflect one's national loyalties, but sombreness actually seems inscribed into the place itself. It foreshadows the uncompromising annihilation of the second war (something which Hitler himself may have been alert to when he visited Langemark in June 1940). It stands on the site of the first mass use of gas in warfare. It does not attempt to make the results of modern warfare 'seemly'. There is an uncompromising honesty about this not terribly well-tended space near Ypres.[9]

The French cemeteries produce other effects. Like the German cemeteries they are typically gathered spaces containing vast numbers of dead. However, unlike Langemark, a site like Notre Dame de Lorette, near Arras, works as a national site of sacrifice, commemoration and thanksgiving. It is the world's largest French military cemetery and it holds 40,000 soldiers, including the ashes of many concentration camp victims from World War Two. In addition to the classic crosses used by the French, the site contains an ossuary, a basilica and other memorial buildings. Of all the memorial spaces I've visited it is the one which most seeks to command the visitor, to determine his or her response most totally. It wishes to set its meaning in a totalising way. We are effectively commanded to bow our heads and know that we are on sacred soil – not simply in the sense of earth which has been consecrated to the Lord, but one which has been consecrated forty thousand times over by the blood of France. The martyrs are martyrs to a vision of France as sacral earth. It is a pure – or perhaps that should be most compromised – meeting point of the sacred and secular. It is a performance of remembrance that is perhaps only possible for a State that has formally separated its connection with the sacred and yet, in the face of deep trauma, must recover its Catholic past to present a future. As a production of memory, the French cemeteries reflect the simple fact that – on the Western Front – it was France (and, of course, a section of Belgium) that was the theatre of death and mutilation. France had to come to a reckoning with mind-boggling levels of slaughter. For example, on 22 August 1914, France lost 27,000 men. As Philip Jenkins notes, 'one single August day cost half as many lives as the United States lost in the entire Vietnam War.'[10] The land and the people are one in mutilation and violation and their recovery and remembrance cannot be separated. One must die without the resurrection of the other.

Perhaps an encounter with French and German cemeteries is necessary for a full appreciation of the quiet effects of the majority of the Commonwealth graveyards.

Yes, there are some extraordinarily lonely little British graveyards. Hidden away up tracks, away from the main pilgrimage routes, these places must be extraordinarily bleak at some points in the year. Equally, some of the larger cemeteries and memorials like the Loos Memorial and, especially, Tyne Cot near Passchendaele have an overwhelming effect that has a family resemblance to a place like Notre Dame de Lorette. And, yet, even Tyne Cot – the largest Commonwealth war cemetery in the world with over 11,000 graves – enacts a different narrative to the 'sacral sacrifice' of French mega-cemeteries. The use of uniform white stone lends Tyne Cot and similar spaces the feel of a Protestant rather than Catholic space, much as the whitewashed walls of post-Reformation churches replaced the rich visual culture of

Catholic churches in many parts of Europe. The mood is of garden, an Imperial garden, but a garden nonetheless. The garden effect – suggestive of the English obsession with tending a plot of land for visual and restful effect – invites the visitor to contemplation. The artifice of the Commonwealth graveyards generates, most of all, a pathetic truth (in the proper sense): this is England or Australia, but ultimately mostly England sunk into 'foreign' earth. England's 'flower' has been cut and grafted into Europe's soil. And so – *pace* the imperial-romantic line of Brooke, 'there is a corner of a foreign field...' – it is an Imperial vision. But the fact of the deaths – that there are so many – already undermines the confidence the Imperial Mind wishes to present. If *this* is what empire looks like – the endless white gravestones and memorials, the million dead – then let us have done with it. Empire kills itself even as it makes its claim.

Yet, if the authorised mood of the British cemeteries is towards 'reflection', 'rest' and 'tranquillity', things moved more slowly in the English countryside. If urban dwellers had increasingly been buried in large municipal cemeteries or even been cremated, in the country, the church graveyard retained its traditional role. I doubt if folk held to medieval notions of Final Judgment or even the desire to be close to the comfort of the church. The church was simply part of life and death. It offered ways of mediating the cycle of life – of birth, marriage and death – and being buried in the churchyard is what one would do when that journey came to a close. Grandad and Granny Collins are both buried in the local churchyard, though neither were noticeably religious. Even in these days of cremation, many folk from my village choose to have their ashes buried in the churchyard and a small memorial raised. My relatives, including Granny and Grandad Mann, are buried in churchyards all over Worcestershire. The world of the village may have evolved out of all recognition since the medieval age when the churchyard would not only have been a place for the dead, but also the place for a marriage to be solemnised. But it retained and, in some ways, retains its glamour as a final resting place.

In 1919, the church was not what it had been a hundred years before, but in a place like the one I grew up in, it was – along with the pub – still a hub for community. Where else would a memorial to the disappeared go? Throughout the war, shrines to the dead had appeared in many of the towns and communities devastated by the war. As with the wayside shrines of our modern age, they might take the form of flowers or a cross with a name. Rolls of honour like the one in Trafford Grove – many of which appeared during the war itself – began to take on the character of the sacred. Indeed, Bushaway claims that 'street shrines represented a growing disaffection with the usual forms of spiritual comfort and solace provided by the Church in the case of bereavement.'[11] But in a place like my home village, the knot was not yet quite severed. Perhaps the bonds of community still went too deep. The place to tell the story of loss was on sacred ground. Every name added to the village memorial would, in life, have been a significant prop of a world which comprised a few hundred souls. Even if they had not been churchgoers, they would have been held over the great stone font as a new-born and, if they'd found a partner, married at the altar. Without repatriation, the village war dead were denied the expectation of their rural lives: burial in the churchyard. Talk of the glorious dead may have been easy and cheap. Honouring lost friends and family would not be.

It is a measure of the grief generated by the Great War that local memorials took the shape they typically did. The overwhelming mood of memorials – urban and rural, civic and church – was solemn remembrance of sacrifice. If people have sometimes sought to co-opt remembrance of the dead for patriotic ends, one of the extraordinary features of the language of remembrance that emerged at this time was its supra-national and mythic character. This was in contrast to the patriotic mood of some European memorials. Furthermore, the character of Remembrance Sunday – overlaid with Kipling's words, 'Lest we forget' – stood in stark contrast to Australia's Anzac Day which celebrated the 'formation of a nation' at Gallipoli in1915. 'The dominant theme [of British memorialisation] was that of sacrifice for the greater good,' notes Bushaway before drawing a conclusion we'd do well to remember: 'This interpretation of Britain's war losses constrained the development of popular socio-political criticisms of post-war conditions.'[12]

For the war had placed civilians into an entirely new relationship with soldiering. The war deaths – unlike those of the colonial wars – were not simply of those who had chosen that profession; suddenly the army was swollen with the ranks of volunteers and the conscripted. The families of this civilian force needed to make sense of their service and deaths in another country. They could not comprehend how a father, brother or son could not be honoured or remembered for what they'd offered. To make lists of those in service – the rolls of honour, for example – became at first a badge of celebration and honour and ended up becoming signs of remembrance. In short, 'The desire to list the names of the fallen arose with the concept of the volunteer army.'[13] But this ensured one thing – that post-war Britain would obsess about who was absent and how they would be memorialised. Talk of sacrifice was unavoidable, but it ensured a paralysis in a proper appreciation of the land Britain had become and the socio-economic issues it faced.

The wayside cross of remembrance, the large and small cenotaphs and the plaques on walls are so much part of the fabric of the nation that we forget that this was not always the 'memorialising' mood following a war. On Chapel Street in Salford and in St Ann's Square Manchester – among many other places – are two memorials to other ways of remembering. I suggest that, to eyes accustomed to Great War Memorials, they present a shocking representation of remembrance. Each is topped by a soldier. But unlike the sombre and determined bronzes created by Great War and Worcestershire Regiment veteran Charles Jagger after the First World War, these soldiers represent barely contained rejoicing. Each is frozen in a moment of throwing his bearskin hat into the air. They are memorials to the Boer War, expressing the mood of deliverance and triumph Britain felt at coming through that war. We live in another time. Yet – as a measure of the extent to which we still live under the shadow of the Great War – we very much understand the mood of solemn remembrance engendered by the Great War. We do not understand the mood of those earlier memorials.

The mood of the Boer War memorials escapes us. They structure memory and remembrance in an alien way. There is something embarrassing about them. They are hard to look at and very difficult to pay attention to for any length of time. They represent Imperial Triumphalism and the sense of deliverance an insecure nation felt, expressed most famously in the rejoicing over the relief of Mafeking. Despite these memorials imposing size and solidity, the Boer War memorials are almost weightless and small. They are hagiographies to Victorian self-satisfaction. In 1910, the Royal Artillery memorial to the South African campaign was unveiled on the Mall. A winged horse representing Peace controls a horse which represents the Spirit of War. Contrast that with Charles Jagger's Royal Artillery memorial unveiled in 1925, depicting a 9.2 Howitzer in stone. 'Fifteen years and 50,000 [Royal Artillery] Great War dead separate these two monuments.'[14] Those deaths sealed a different approach.

Curiously, the Boer War memorials signal just how incommensurate the Great War was for the English imperial mind. The Boer War lasted almost three years. During that time about 20,000 British soldiers died, 13,000 as a result of disease. It was a serious and major conflict, involving half a million Imperial troops. Boer military casualties counted about 10,000 dead and civilian casualties – including victims of British concentration camps – may have been between 50 and 100,000 if one includes the (typical of the time) uncounted deaths of black Africans. If Britain had lost in South Africa, the great power's imperial image would have been seriously bashed. But – ultimately – the Boer War was a colonial war. It was a war for which Britain's peacetime army was made. It was – despite some of the lessons on show about the power of the machine gun, for example – a nineteenth-century war.

Yet if they are bewildering, there is an ironic sense in which the Boer War memorials are full of pathos. For their presumed mood of rejoicing and celebration and thanksgiving for deliverance are revealed as utterly naïve when placed in the context of what the Empire faced little more than a decade later. During the Battle of the Somme, 20,000 British soldiers died in one day. Over one hundred years on from the Boer War, the mood of its memorials is simply bewildering. For British society has – partly in the light of the Great War – become so thoroughly ironic that many of us are inclined to see the real heroes of the Great War as those who refused to fight, who refused the passivity and submissiveness that became a primary mode of the war. Our heroes are the deserters, the ones who refused to have things done to them, who rejected 'self-sacrifice' as the way of being. In 1994, in Tavistock Square a memorial was unveiled 'to all who have established and are maintaining the right to refuse to kill. Their foresight and courage give us hope.'

It is a startling trajectory. Aristotle famously takes the soldier as his model of the virtue of courage. There are good reasons for this. If E. M. Forster hoped that if he had had to make a choice between betraying his country or his friend, he would choose his country, I suspect soldiers would be cautious about the dichotomy. One of the repeated statements of soldiers I've known is that, when it comes down to it, they fight for their mates. They are capable of making the most startling demonstrations of courage for the sake of their friends, even unto laying down their lives. There is also a case to be made that they witness to a world that is more important than self-preservation. A soldier witnesses to a reality that some things, some principles are worth dying for. Yet our modern heroes tend to be those whose courage is demonstrated in resistance to authority and the command – even when we seek to dress it up with Just War rhetoric – to kill. As Geoff Dyer claims, 'the deserter's grave has become a hero's grave; pride has come to reside not in the carrying out of duty but in its humane dereliction.'[15]

It is sobering to remember, one hundred years on from the Great War, that almost all the markers of remembrance were based on public subscription rather than state aid. Individuals and communities shaped their grief around the memorials raised and the nation had never seen so many cairns of memorial made. There was a frenzy of memorialisation. The stillness of the resultant memorials like the one in my home church's graveyard contrasted strikingly with the civic energies poured into many of the projects. While the need to have foci for unprecedented levels of grief and sacrifice was clearly a key motor for this energy, it takes very little wit to imagine others. If the energies were sincere, equally the need to make some response to the incomprehensible and terrible is also a basic human need. In our own time, road deaths – especially of the young – are greeted by way-side shrines of flowers and messages; lighting a candle, either in a church or as part of a vigil has become part of the emotional response of the religious and non-religious alike. The war memorials of England were the last flowering of Victorian religiosity, imperial pride and civic surety. If those who had returned from the fighting often felt awkward around them – Sam and Bert were never to be seen at Remembrance Sunday or Armistice Day parades – or if veterans were initially unpopular (sometimes the suspicion was mutual), perhaps it was because they got in the way of the civilians' task. The returning heroes were not the dead heroes. They were not the glorious dead.

Not least among the striking truths about the majority of church and civic, of rural and urban, memorials is their potent uselessness. There are exceptions to this – St Matthew's Stretford, where I served as curate, is not alone in having a chapel dedicated to the memory of a beloved son killed in the carnage, a kind of protestant version of a chantry. But remembrance was shaped around the non-utilitarian. Memorials were just that – memorials.[17] The contrast with the response to the Second World

War could not be more startling. Clearly there are a number of factors which ought not to be ignored here. Firstly, the *matériel* and language of remembrance were already well established come 1945. The memorial stones had already been erected – all that was necessary in a village like the one I grew up in was to add further names from another conflict.

There was also the simple fact that the nation was materially damaged in a way that it had not been in 1918. If the Great War had been marked by vast divisions between the front and home, in the second war being at home could still mean being on the front line. While in the second war, soldiers and civilians might still be separated for years at a time,[17] one of the key marks of the Great War was the extraordinary contrast between the home and front-line experience. Writers like Graves and Sassoon repeatedly comment upon it. In 1916, R.H. Tawney, back in Blighty with wounds, wrote in *The Nation*, about 'the people with whom I really am at home, the England that's not an island or an empire, but a wet populous dyke stretching from Flanders to the Somme.' Charles Loch Mowat concludes that in 1919, 'Most things, and most people in politics, were all too familiar. Mark Abrams has well pointed out that anyone who knew the England of 1914 would find little superficial change by 1939: the same names on the front of chain stores, the same newspapers owned by the same press lords ... the traveller who journeyed back to 1914 would meet then, in the prime of life, half the members of parliament of 1939.'[18]

The Second World War had a different character to the First. Vast areas of London and other urban centres were damaged and destroyed by bombing; almost no part of the country escaped being militarised in some sense. Rationing was experienced by all. In a very real way, Britain understood that the second war was a conflict for national survival. The war came very close to home. The need to rebuild the nation was a genuine impulse in the memorialising instinct of combatant and civilian alike. The instinct to renew and re-imagine the national and local community was reflected in the landslide victory for the Labour

Party. Churchill, the leader who had helped deliver the nation, was – to his bewilderment – ejected from power. The spirit of the age was communitarian. In our village a new parish hall was erected and dedicated to the community. The generation who fought and worked together for six years in the 1940s were determined not to return to an old world of privilege and injustice. The Great War for Civilisation had failed to be the war to end war; it had not led to a 'Land Fit For Heroes'. After the Second War things had to be different. The old dispensation would not work.

But I will not mock the memorialising instinct of an earlier generation. The theologian and poet in me is attentive to the power of the useless and non-utilitarian. Precisely what is most potent about the Christian liturgy is its abiding uselessness. It does not exist to appease or influence God. It does not 'function' to make us better or holier or more committed. Nor is it a kind of ritual magic or invocation. It is a recapitulation of what makes the Christian community the community it is – a community of atonement. It is the rehearsal of the story of God that illuminates and sustains the world. That story is that God is Love and liturgy is one way we participate in this truth-claim and grow to be ourselves. Breaking bread and wine, making confession and so on is us being ourselves together. When liturgy is put to practical ends – to make us feel happy for example – it misses truth, which is to be in proper relationship with the Divine. As I've noted elsewhere,[19] a mystic like Meister Eckhart understood that 'to use God is to kill him'. When we put God to our ends and uses – as indeed the likes of Bishop Winnington-Ingram sought to do during the Great War – what we are left with is not God, but an idol or simulacrum shaped in our image. God always escapes and exceeds our utilitarian strategies and living liturgy is precisely an encounter with that truth. Liturgy undoes our strategies of control and utility and exposes us to the Divine Love. And if there is anything to be learned from love it is humility – to see ourselves for who and what we are and commit ourselves to wholeness.

It is possible to attempt to present the memorial culture and the rituals which accrued to them (the two-minute silence, the poppy wreaths, etc.) in a functional way. One can see them as attempts to mediate and solemnise the pain and loss – to imbue the terrible with some sort of meaning. Talk of 'the glorious dead' or of 'life sacrificed for future generations' are obvious examples of a species of cultural power which seeks to find transcendent meaning in war. In cultures deeply grounded in Christianity there is a clear co-option of Christian talk for the purposes of politics, though talk of honour and sacrifice and glory clearly have classical antecedents. At a crude level, one might suggest that the co-option of concepts like 'sacrifice' by the powerful and comfortable in society is a strategy of control or self-justification. How can one 'sell' the deaths of the best part of a million to a grieving nation except by making use of the language of glory and honour? For the sake of community survival, meaning must be recovered from the meaningless.

The complication is that we cannot always control the signs we make or use. If a narrative of utility can be made to work around the post-Great War memorials and rituals – either as a conscious or more realistically as an unconscious cultural impulse – the mode of remembrance is significant. Almost exclusively the local and national communities did not look to make practical things – railway stations, village halls, hospitals. Perhaps things might have been better if they had. The so-called 'Land fit for heroes' might have had a greater chance of realisation; perhaps an early creation of an NHS or comprehensive social care system might have not only spared the indignities of the 1930s, but have helped heal a divided nation. Rather, communities reached for a kind of secular liturgy. And given some of the inflated, vengeful rhetoric around at the War's close – no doubt stoked up by the need to win a General Election – we should be glad. The likes of trade unionist and future Labour MP G.N. Barnes could say, without apology, 'Well, I'm for hanging the Kaiser.' The *Daily Mail* published, in a box on the front page, each day, the totals of British casualties, trying to keep the demand for vengeance at fever heat. The allies famously exacted their own financial vengeance with notorious long-term consequences. Yet at a local level, the memorials offered a different focal point than brute revenge. The memorials were like a stone pall laid over the nation. In a way in which we cannot now imagine, the nation had become a liminal place where ghosts – of the imagination, of the past and a lost future – walked in the presence of a broken present.

I have officiated at almost countless funerals, including some tragic cases of lives cut short. These services can be extraordinarily charged. They can be said to have a practical dimension – to enable or guide the grieving through liminal states. The priest and the liturgy guide the grieving through the emotional, spiritual and psychological edge-lands of human being and identity. Like Charon guiding the dead to Hades, the liturgy helps to take the living across the lake of grief. After the Great War, individuals, families and communities needed means to begin to negotiate the incomprehensible. The rituals of remembrance and their memorialised focal points were unprecedented attempts to find a way across the shadows between life and death.

But often life is a matter of both/and, rather than either/or. If these seemingly practical and utilitarian considerations cannot be dismissed neither can I doubt the power of uselessness. As with funerals I have been privileged to officiate at, I see how the liturgy and actions – the casting of flowers into the grave for example – and so on are about helping mourners 'move on'. But I have also witnessed the way the grieving sometimes just need to stare and be silent and witness to the appalling truth of reality – that those who were living are now gone. I have sat in vigil – either by the coffin, or, later on, by a headstone – with parents who have lost young children. And we have stared and not understood. And there is nothing to say. For all there is to look at is terror or the terrible or nothingness. And nothing will make it better. And yet we have still looked and borne witness. And waited in bewilderment.

If grief is the price we all pay for living well and if many of us have wrestled with the shape of loss, I am not sure any of us in the UK can quite imagine what those months and years after the Great War were quite like. For millions of survivors – both combatant and civilian – the solid ground of living had been torn up in Flanders and Picardy. Their children, brothers, friends had set sail for the land of the dead. All they saw when they looked around were the absent dead. Those who were left behind were alone in their grief and yet it was the one thing they shared with neighbours, friends and complete strangers. If the world had come loose from its traditional anchors should we be surprised if they sought to use weighty stone and marble to find stillness again?

CHAPTER SEVEN

'Wounds' – The impact of 'shell-shock' on masculinity in a time of psychiatry

In Francois Dupeyron's 2001 film adaptation of *The Officer's Ward*, Eric Caravaca plays Adrien, a dashing French officer severely wounded during France's first engagement of the Great War. Unlike the source novel, the film concentrates on the period spent by Adrien in hospital and emphasises the horror of his injuries. On Adrien's arrival at the ward, all the mirrors are removed and staff are instructed not to give any to him, but we see from the expressions on the faces of others just how bad the damage is. Adrien becomes increasingly desperate to see the damage done to his face, even asking a visitor to draw a picture of him. Dupeyron ensures that we do not see the horrifying extent of Adrien's injuries until the moment that he himself does – by looking at his reflection in a window pane. It is for him a moment of revelation and revaluation. Revelation because he sees what – in visual terms – he has become; revaluation because he begins to comprehend that he will be judged on the basis of what Sartre termed 'le regard des autres' or 'the look of the other'. That is, instead of being understood for his actions and character he will – like a woman typically is – be judged on the basis of his appearance. And his looks, like that of a terrifying monster, will repel and terrify or cause stares.[1] He has become objectified and 'othered'; he has become one who is measured by what can be seen in a reflection rather than someone who knows what he is through action and ownership of space. In a world which 'judges' on the basis of the visual, he has become, in short, not fully human. He has become 'monstrous'. He has become 'other'.

One of the powerful threads in Pat Barker's *Regeneration* trilogy is a speculation that one of the 'wounds' inflicted upon fighting men in the Great War was a kind of 'feminisation'. Rivers,[2] the psychiatrist, (as Barker's vox) wonders whether the conditions in the trenches – constricting, forcing men to inaction and passivity, living a life with no control (and expecting death any moment) – have pushed men into the traditional position of women. Barker asks whether men – raised to conceive of themselves as 'active', 'dynamic' and owners of space – have been forced into the condition of the 'done to' rather than 'the doing'. Clearly, behind this speculation is a lot of psycho-dynamic and feminist re-reading of soldiers' experiences. In short, Barker wonders whether the soldiers' experience of 'shell-shock' was akin to what psychiatrists then considered to be the 'female problem' – hysteria. As Ben Shephard in his history of military psychiatry argues, we should be careful about too readily accepting Barker's account: 'Pat Barker would have us believe that by 1918 officer-patients in shell-shock hospitals were discussing the finer points of Freudian doctrine with each other.'[3]

Yet if one would wish to bring considerable critical force to bear on Barker's 1990s feminist speculations about the impact of trench warfare on masculinity, the Great War constructed a novel language of wounds and woundedness. A new and disturbing term – 'shell-shock' – was coined (first used in medical discourse in *The Lancet* in 1915 by pioneering military psychiatrist Charles Myer) to begin to give some account of the impact of static, high-explosive war on human subjectivity. For, by December 1914, alarming reports had reached the War Office in London of at least 7–10 per cent of officers and 3–4 per cent of other ranks being withdrawn from the front line with 'nervous and mental shock'. These were no half-trained civilians. These were men drawn from the professional army, who had been shaped for combat often over ten to fifteen years. Yet as Ben Shephard claims, 'Shell-shock was an early example of a common medical phenomenon: a medical debate, hedged with scientific qualifications, taken up by public opinion and the media in an oversimplified way.'[4] In cultural contexts learning new languages about violence, it was unsurprising that public and media interest in a novel widespread phenomenon would be high. Newspapers as restrained as *The Times* began to speak of 'wounds of consciousness' or 'the wounded mind'. In late 1915, the Army Council for the first time officially acknowledged that there was a grey area between cowardice and madness. Military and political discourse about 'soldiering' as an icon of masculinity was beginning to shift.

Dr Chaim Shatan, a psychiatrist who worked extensively with Vietnam vets in the 1970s and was one of the group who brought 'Post-Traumatic Stress Disorder' into common diagnostic use, famously quipped, 'Military psychiatry is to psychiatry as military music is to music.' This was never clearer than in the Great War. Military medicine – always a servant of the war juggernaut – struggled to come to terms with not only fractured bodies, but traumatised subjects. Even as the Army Council began to acknowledge that a man's refusal and/or inability to fight might not be cowardice, medics were caught in a diagnostic mess. The army in France was instructed to distinguish between 'Shell-Shock, W' (where it was 'clear' that symptoms were caused by combat) and 'Shell-Shock, S' (for 'sickness', where symptoms may have developed later). This distinction mattered not least because being put in the latter category deprived a soldier of a wound-stripe, a pension and, of course, honour and respect. Without 'wound' status a soldier might be told to pull himself together and be sent back to the front, or shot for cowardice. By all accounts, front-line medicine – often practised under fire and in unsanitary, pressured conditions – struggled to interpret the Army Council's new diktat and doctors continued to routinely label patients 'Mental', 'Insane' or even 'GOK' (God Only Knows).

As the war progressed it became clear that 'Shell-Shock' was an utterly inadequate term for what was happening to large numbers of soldiers as a result of front-line service. Pioneers like Charles Myers and Harold Wiltshire who treated soldiers at Base Hospitals in France began to appreciate that the 'nervous' and physical symptoms displayed by soldiers could not be accounted for in terms of a mechanical relationship between 'shell-blast' and the proximity of the human body. As Myers put it twenty years after the war, '"shell-shock" does not depend for [its] causation on the physical force (or the chemical effects) of the bursting shell.' In June 1916, Myers – the man who'd coined the term 'shell-shock' – proposed it should be abandoned by the Army and replaced by two conditions called 'concussion' and 'nervous shock'.

If, as theorist Elaine Scarry has suggested, the primary function of war is injuring – that is, to cause damage to human bodies so that they cannot be effective – not least among war's other effects is its capacity to disrupt meaning. Indicative of this truth is the Great War's impact on the language of nerve and nerves. In short, the association of 'nerve' with courage, masculinity and virility was – after years of violence – definitively shifted into the language of 'nerves' and nervousness. Certainly as early as 1894 the *Spectator* magazine noted the shifted meaning of the words 'nerve' and 'nervous'. In mid-Victorian discourse, the 'nervous man' had been a person whose strength was well strung and under control. The magazine speculated that the shift towards associating 'nervousness' with 'a timidity that borders on cowardice' reflected an increasing strain on men, not least in the form of 'fast' and decadent living. The *Spectator* raised that common refrain at the heart of any insecure patriarchal culture: men were becoming 'softer'. Men were being encouraged to 'talk' about their 'nerves' to doctors as they never had before. The magazine concluded, 'between popular folly and the indulgent doubts of doctors, nervous disorders are making far greater strides among us than the stress of modern life would really justify.'

If, in 1894, the *Spectator* rehearsed a common patriarchal theme – the decline of manliness in the 'present' age and the rise of 'feminisation' – the conditions of the trenches provided acute conditions for the exposure of patriarchal masculinity's limits. In August 1915, Lieutenant Anthony Alfands wrote of the trench 'experience': 'You sit like rabbits in a burrow and just wait for something to come and blow you to hell.' The image of 'rabbit' could not be further away from classic martial metaphors. These soldiers are not lions or tigers. They are not predators. They are not demi-gods like Achilles. They are rabbits in a hole. Alfands adds, 'It gets on your nerves always waiting for the next bang. If one or two land unpleasantly near one's fore trench the usual effect is that you imagine every other shell is coming around and about the same place ... nerves seem to be the one vital thing for a soldier ... and better still no nerves.' As Charles Wilson, a medical officer for the 1/Royal Fusiliers, said, 'The acid test of a man in the trenches was high explosive. It taught us things about ourselves we had not known till then.' For many, it taught them the limits of traditional masculinity. The historian Ben Shephard tells another story of a soldier admitted to a Maida Vale hospital in January 1915 who had completely lost his memory after being blown up by a shell near Ypres in October 1914. He had been sent first to a hospital in Manchester and now spoke with a Lancashire accent. But under hypnosis he regained his memory and spoke in his native Wiltshire accent. He could describe the appalling experience of being under bombardment. But when he came out of hypnosis he could remember nothing and spoke again in a 'Manc' accent. After twenty-five hypnosis sessions doctors admitted 'failure' and the man was discharged as a case of lost personality.[5]

One horizon of the late Victorian and Edwardian 'crisis' in masculinity was the notion of 'Christian manliness.' The power of this narrative was grounded in its resilience and evolution over many centuries. Arguably it emerged in its early military form in the High Middle Ages when agrarian feudal culture – structured around authority, stratified power and divine warrant – coalesced around pictures of the knight as 'holy warrior' serving Christ through arms, courage and crusade. Its evolution in Western European cultures was guaranteed by the adaptive skills of the ruling classes. The landed gentry and aristocracy were inclined to define their values – and therefore, as ruling class, wider society's values – in terms of military skill and maintaining 'readiness' for war through martial activities like hunting, fencing and shooting. Indeed, as Isabel Colegate's 1980 novel *The Shooting Party* suggests, the European ruling class's vigorous commitment to the Great War lay in part in its obsession with ritualised violence like hunting and shooting. The Shooting Party that takes place in the novel in 1913 is a foreshadowing of the violence that is to come the following year.[6]

By the nineteenth century, the public schools emerged as the repositories for the English ruling class's representation of its ideal self-image to itself. The emergent upper-middle classes provided a means to disseminate that self-image. As wealthy middle-class and upper-middle-class families began to send their sons to major and minor public schools, an ideology shaped around character and manliness was disseminated. And, even in an era when Christianity was under greater questioning than ever before (through the twin poles of industrialisation and science), 'Christian Character' in men was idealised as central to Victorian Imperial confidence. The 1864 Clarendon Commission claimed, 'The English people were indebted to these schools,' not least for 'their capacity to govern others and control themselves ... their vigour and manliness of character ... their love of healthy sports and exercise.'

This was a context in which Christianity was not obviously or ordinarily associated with quietism and pacifism. In 1867, William Booth founded the Salvation Army, an organisation structured around military ranks and colours or flags, with music that often had the character of folk marching tunes. If its focus was (and is) on serving and 'saving' the poorest and most vulnerable in society by offering a militarily-structured discipline, it may strike us as extraordinary now that God was so confidently associated with military concepts in the nineteenth century. Organisations like the Boys' Brigade, the Lads' Drill Associations and, in Edwardian England, the Boy Scouts sought to bring Christian manliness to the working-classes. If they might have had greater appeal to lower-middle boys than the urban poor, nonetheless they offered a sense of adventure, physical achievement and patriotic faith which mirrored some of the Public School Ethos. The 'Stiff-Upper Lip' became one of, if not *the* defining performance of English masculinity in the late nineteenth and early twentieth century; not least of the indications of this truth was how it was written 'against' both in the decadent literature of the *fin de siècle* and in the Edwardian novels of E.M. Forster, which explored the power of passion in the face of emotional repression.

One of the central tropes generated about the Great War *by* the Great War was the pall of personal 'silence'. That is, the War's 'disappearance' from personal discourse. Those who had witnessed the worst of battle famously did not talk about it post-war. My grandfathers were living examples of the trope. They were parsimonious with the details of their respective wars. They were hardly loquacious men at the best of times, but about the War they mostly refused to speak. In so many ways it was a war fought to be remembered rather than be talked about. Early in the war this trajectory was not yet fully established. The famous poster from 1914–15, 'Daddy, what did you do in the Great War?' imagined a future in which a young girl quizzed her troubled, non-combatant father about his involvement in the conflict. The look on the father's face is a mixture of anxiety and shame. The poster constructs a picture of a post-war in which men will be interrogated by small children about their courage or lack of it. It anticipates that it may be the kind of conflict which could be talked about. Yet, outside of literary memoir, military history and the fiftieth anniversary landmark TV series *The Great War* – that is, outside of 'public performance' – it was not. It was a war which lacked the structure of 'personal reminiscence'. This war did not have the structure of Crimea or the Boer War in which old/er soldiers might reminisce over old triumphs and victories with their chums.

In short, the war itself became the trauma to be repressed. This is not to deny the very real, material trauma inflicted on men like my grandfathers. Grandad Bert had a leg wound that never truly healed. Inoperable pieces of shrapnel were lodged in one of his legs. My mum tells of how at least once a month the wound would flare up, suppurate and confine him to bed for a few days. Grandad Sam's issues were more emotional. His moods and temper belonged to the category we'd now call Post-Traumatic Stress Disorder (PTSD). By the end of the Great War the British army had dealt with at least 80,000 cases of shell-shock. Some of these men would never recover. Others, like the poet-composer Ivor Gurney would alternate between lucidity and collapse. The British wounded totalled in the region of one and a half million. Damaged bodies were everywhere and families were affected for generations. Yet, when placed in a post-war context where most simply wanted to get on with rediscovering narratives of normality and ordinariness, such trauma was almost unavoidably repressed. If Pat Barker's 1990s revisionism takes the Freudian claims too far, this was, nonetheless, the first major war fought in a time of psychiatry and psychotherapy. New constructions of language which are also new ways of talking about 'self' and 'identity' emerged. Repression, denial, the Subconscious and the Unconscious and so on, reconstructed the cultural and subjective landscape.

As I've quoted elsewhere, Edmund Blunden said, of the Somme, 'the war had won and would keep on winning.' If the War was not to win post-war it was hardly surprising if it was repressed as Other, as dangerous and monstrous. In over thirty eight million cases[7] the war had shown itself to be the terrifying Other of 'civilisation' and 'culture'. Specifically, it was the definitive threat to the patriarchal-masculine constructed subject. This was and is 'the subject' which defines and determines 'reality', which shapes the world according to 'his' will and desires. This masculine subject is defined as being in charge and control, who claims the position of privilege and 'power-over', often with divine warrant. On this picture, men are not simply dominant in virtue of tradition or 'nature', but because divine texts say they are. At its most obvious and crude (yet still potent), the warrant is found in texts like the Bible which place men, represented by the likes of Adam, first in creation.

War has classically been seen as that most macho endeavour. It is *the* test of masculinity. Yet, ironically, the particular nature of the Great War might be read as 'feminine'. Its particular structure – leaving men cowering in trenches, waiting to be destroyed by high explosive, unable to use displays of courage to genuinely break the deadlock – deprived men of the 'active' masculine position Western culture set them up to occupy.[8] War has so often been seen the ultimate test of manhood, indeed as the final way a man may prove himself and complete himself. Yet, the Great War's dominant structure threatened that. As psychodynamic thinkers like Freud and Lacan have argued, femininity represents – conceptually – both 'threat' to masculinity and the means by which masculinity has asserted its privilege and power. Femininity represents castration, lack and absence, yet simultaneously masculinity uses that 'lack' as a way of asserting its difference. It is the 'Other' which masculinity uses to define its normative status. Scholars like Elisabeth Bronfen[9] have further indicated that 'femininity' on these terms has typically been identified with the ultimate 'Other', 'Death'. War always intersects with masculinity's deepest terror: its annihilation in death. The Feminine, the Other, Death itself threaten to overwhelm and generates terror. Yet, the Great War – principally understood as a war which was dominated by stasis and powerlessness in the face of high-explosive – doubles this threat. Not only is death threatened, but men are deprived of the means by which to face it 'like a man'. He is reduced to being done to rather than doing.

War, even for its survivors, leaves its marks on its participants in the form of wounds – the wounded 'mind' and the wounded body and the Great War rewrote the scale and language of wounds. The wounded man lost his patriarchal position of power; the man with the wounded 'mind' even more so. For, as many philosophers from Plato to Kant have suggested, masculinity and the male has been hugely and readily identified with 'Mind' and 'Thought', unlike women who have commonly been over-identified with 'Body'. A man with a damaged 'mind' was endlessly open to accusations of shirking and cowardice, that is, of weakness. And in the Great War this othering of the wounded – in body and mind – was effected in millions of cases across Europe. Like Adrien in *The Officers' Ward*, the wounded were brought into a condition closer to a woman. They were, as the Latin root of wound, 'vulnus', reminds us, vulnerable and no longer self-sufficient. They lived as an exposure of the frailty of patriarchally-conceived masculinity.

Among the most sensitive and evocative studies of the effects of 'shell-shock', repression and trauma on the masculine subject is J.L. Carr's 1980 Booker-nominated, *A Month in the Country*.[10] Set in North Yorkshire in the summer of 1920, it revolves around the friendship between two men, Birkin and Moon. Both are traumatised veterans and each has come to the village of Oxgodby for work: Birkin to uncover a 500-year-old wall painting on the village church and Moon to find the lost Medieval grave of a notable local resident. Both the novel and the beautiful 1987 film adaptation, starring Colin Firth and Ken Branagh, are at their strongest when presenting the simple dissonance between the men's recent past and people's desire to get on with their lives, amid the beauty of the English countryside. The film has panorama after panorama of rolling hills unsullied by violence. It might easily be the fields of Northern France, except we know that they have been recently destroyed by high explosive. The Vicar and his wife, the local gentry, as well as the humble people of 'The Chapel' try to get on with their lives as if it were still 1913. Yet the War as repressed 'other' refuses to remain hidden despite many people's best efforts. A farmer and his wife speak plaintively of their son killed in the war. A young girl dying from TB shows that 'the monstrous' simply will not go away despite the idyllic setting. Birkin and Moon scream at night. Indeed, Moon has dug a trench inside his tent in which he sleeps. Room enough for one man. A 'trench' that also represents his grave.

Over the summer the two men begin to heal, not least through a process of 'substitution' – they find in their respective work a place to negotiate their pain. They expose their trauma by allowing their work to speak 'into' them and their trauma into their work. For Birkin it is in the slow work of revealing a medieval 'Judgment' Wall in the Church. He slowly exposes an artist's rendering of a world-view long since lost, both figuratively and literally, to the modern world. In it the Church represents not the Post-Reformation 'whitewashed' walls of hope and salvation, but the promise of ultimate judgment. He uncovers a pre-literate, visual world where the attention is not centred on the written 'Word of God' – the Bible – but on visual representations of a fixed world where Christ judges, the righteous are saved and the wicked are damned for all time. As Moon says to Birkin as the image of Jesus is revealed, 'there is no mercy in your Christ.'

For Birkin, the atheist, there is healing to be found in acting as servant to the artist who made the masterwork on the wall. Birkin's judgment – knowing when too little of the whitewash has been stripped off, when too much – is harnessed to serving a community's picture of Universal Judgement. More than that, he begins to find healing as his craftsman's knife exposes and comes into relationship with a world older and deeper than the traumatised reality he has so recently lived through. He places his shattered narrative in another story, one that is uncompromising and ancient. For Moon, a war hero who was sent to prison in the final stages of the war for homosexuality, a kind of healing comes not so much in finding the lost grave he seeks, but finding that its contents are subversive and unexpected. Moon, a man who sleeps in a surrogate grave and who has seen too much death, meets death again in the form of a medieval skeleton. This 'strange meeting' – as Wilfred Owen might put it – makes new 'healing' space available for Moon. For the encounter offers an unexpected revelation: that the body was buried outside holy ground because its owner was a Muslim. On his grave is inscribed, 'I, of all men, the most wretched.' This ancestor of the local landed gentry was no figure of respectability but utterly cast-out as Other. Moon meets his (and his generation's) historical analogue and is no longer quite so afraid of living.

A Month in the Country models, most of all, how the deep trauma of war cannot be made commensurate with 'ordinary' life, but can be reckoned with – in some measure – through relationship. Birkin and Alice Keach, the Vicar's wife, are attracted to each other, but given the social constraints on their lives cannot act on it. Moon and Birkin share a fondness that circles around the erotic, but which neither can act on. Yet, as these people work out the after-effects of a post-Edwardian world destroyed by war, the gentle exposure to each other's vulnerability and need (Mrs Keach is starved of affection by her frosty husband) quietly makes a future possible. There is no return to an age of innocence. As Alice and Birkin walk through some idyllic woods the local squire shoots rabbits and destroys their 'paradise'. But memory and past – forever sullied by violence – slowly reform as less terrifying as the world turns. At one point, Moon says, 'I tell myself it'll get better as time passes and it sinks further back. But it's got nowhere to sink to, has it?' What Moon and Birkin (and the men and women they represent) discover is that if they can find nowhere in their own traumatised minds for the War to sink, it finds a level in the ancient rhythms and unexpected aporia of landscape and narrative.

Exposure to one's vulnerability, especially when one carries around self-images of one's own personal power and completeness can be shattering. The violation of the body and its integrity is trauma and trauma's effects are manifold. To be assaulted, to be tortured and to be injured can be a 'work' of silencing and fragmentation, not least the fragmentation of one's very subjectivity. Sometimes out of that catastrophe of loss emerges a hunger to say the unsayable, to construct new articulations and recover a voice that has (sometimes systematically) been broken. When the body has been used as weapon against its own value and integrity, sometimes the only work that may redeem the appalling is a work of 'resurrection'. And this resurrection is indicated by the fact of 'survival' and in finding new ways of 'articulation'.

The post-war Modernist era – defined in literature by the experiments of Eliot, Pound and Woolf – made some unexpected resurrections available. Many have suggested that the 1920s and 1930s were the Golden Age of Detective Fiction. It has often been read as a conservative format and there are good grounds for that claim. Perhaps the popularity of Ngaio Marsh, Dorothy L. Sayers, Margery Allingham, and above all, Agatha Christie was tied to a desire for escapism. Certainly, even a brief overview of some of the detectives developed by the Queens of Crime – Poirot (the absurd little Belgian), Wimsey (the flaneur-aristo), and Albert Campion (the amateur hiding his privileged past) to name just three – indicate the absurdist element at the heart of their work. Yet, as some scholars have indicated, it's possible to read these texts more substantially. Sayers, in particular, offers a fascinating critical intervention into readings of the Great War and masculinity.

Sayers' famous hero Lord Peter Wimsey offers particular insight into the cultural significance of woundedness and damaged masculinity in the post-war era. At one level, Wimsey represents Sayers' idealised man – brilliant but lazy, foppish but kind, humane and sophisticated, a war hero who took a Blue in cricket whilst at Balliol, yet is self-effacing about his undoubted gifts. In short, the gentleman *manqué*. His honourable and loving pursuit of Harriet Vane's hand in marriage can be read as Sayers' wish-fulfilment. Yet, Sayers – a serious writer about Christianity, a scholar as well as a popular novelist – dares to infuse Wimsey with a striking and unexpected wound: shell-shock. For Wimsey, a former temporary major in the Rifle Brigade, had the terrifying and not uncommon experience of being buried alive in the trenches. In a number of the novels it revisits him in quite devastating form. In a moment of understatement, Peter says to Harriet – now his wife – after a troubled flashback, 'It was just the old responsibility dream.' The impact of a shell-shocked world on masculinity is something Sayers explores convincingly in a number of novels, not least *The Unpleasantness at the Bellona Club* (1928) – in which a suspect in a murder is a shell-shock victim – and Sayers' first novel, *Whose Body?* (1923) in which the effects of Wimsey's shell-shock are honestly, un-sensationally explored.

The critic Monica Lott argues, 'In the medium of detective fiction, Sayers explores issues of crippled masculinity in postwar Britain and offers detection as a treatment for shell-shock, making a strong claim for the power of the genre.'[11] In short, detection offers Wimsey a route to regain the masculinity damaged in the trenches. Lott adds, 'Lord Peter encapsulates the burgeoning Modernist movement through his frustration with authority, particularly that of the police force; his sense of loneliness and alienation when solving a case; and his nostalgia for a simpler time before his war experiences.'[12] Indeed, arguably, one of the marks of detective fiction's success in this era lay in its questioning of governmental authority, its emphasis on the motivation of the individual, and its challenge to social customs. Despite Lord Peter's close friendship with Chief Inspector Charles Parker (who later becomes his brother-in-law, thereby breaking class conventions), his sure-footed genius is what the reader relies on, not the plodding authorities. In a context where traditional authority had been placed under severe strain by the trauma of the war, Wimsey and the other classic detectives reassured readers that someone was keeping order and administering justice.

What is outstanding about Sayers' work is that she invests authority and justice in the figure of a damaged man who grows into and comes to terms with his vulnerability. The wounded man is the locus of authority. Early in his career, Wimsey is balanced carefully between upper-class cool and emotional collapse. Parker exposes Wimsey's temptation to take refuge in that upper-class cool in his pursuit of criminals by stating bluntly, 'Peter ... you can't be a sportsman. You're a responsible person.' Parker reminds Peter that his skills will lead to the death of another human being by hanging. Peter discovers through his relationships with Parker, his valet Bunter, his future wife Harriet and his brother, the Duke of Denver, the limits of post-Edwardian masculine performance. The interactions lead to new performances and exposures. Crucially, Sayers interrogates the concept of 'the detective' – as the one who investigates the world, understands what he sees and brings it under control – as an icon of masculinity. And time and again, the novels expose Wimsey to reminders that – in a time of capital punishment – his 'successes' send men to the gallows just as once he sent men to their deaths on the Western Front. 'The Old Responsibility Dream' is an icon not only of Wimsey's personal trauma, but the wound at the heart of a civilisation based on legitimated violence. Wimsey is allowed to be self-aware of his trauma and weakness. He is not identified with 'Mind' as detective *manqué* Sherlock Holmes is. He is at times made vulnerable by the War's effects and cannot control his emotion. Indeed, as Lott concludes, 'Lord Peter's self-awareness of the weaknesses brought upon him by his war experiences introduces a character whose emotion and detective abilities create an anti-rationality that redefines post-war masculinity.'[13]

The final complete Wimsey novel, *Busman's Honeymoon*, represents, through their marriage, Harriet and Peter's united commitment to the work of healing the world.[14] On their honeymoon this urbane couple return to rural England. This is not only the rural England they both grew up in, but rural England as symbolic of Englishness. Their union – sophisticated, grounded in equality and respect as well as love – will rejuvenate the land itself, a still traumatised England (of which Peter is an icon). While this is a conservative conclusion – Harriet says at one point, 'I have married England' and Peter tells her, 'I have come home' – it dares to offer a conclusion which (as one might expect from a Christian of Sayers' moral seriousness) does not flinch from honesty about the wounds to the post-war body and an England that has tried and failed to move on.

England's failure to move on from the War's trauma is represented in the very bricks and mortar they've bought for their honeymoon and future home. It is a solid country farmhouse, but this promised home is also the site of a murder that must be dealt with before the land can be healed. Most significantly of all, the novel concludes with Peter breaking-down for a final time as the murderer is executed off-stage. It is an ultimate acknowledgement of responsibility, but it also signifies the wounded war hero's coming home. Not to a wife who will serve his every need or be the mother of his children, but to friendship, respect and mutual, equal love between two people who 'see' each other. It's only in relationship that there is hope – in their shared vocation to work, service and justice in a compromised world.

Towards the end of *A Month in the Country*, Moon says to Birkin, 'I don't know if it's worse not having something to show, like a lost limb or two or blindness. I mean people like you and me, the intact ones.' There were, of course, 'intact ones' after the Great War. There were men and women who, by most reasonable measures, went through the conflict physically and emotionally unscathed. But even those who worked a 'cushy number', in the army or elsewhere, could hardly have been said to have remained unaffected. Even if my Grandad Bert hadn't been among the physically wounded, he and his family would have had to reckon with the death of his brother Tom in Egypt. Ripples flowed out from each small incident in the war. And the Land Fit For Heroes was, after four years of relentless conflict, a Land Wounded with Heroes. Not least among the traumas of the Great War was an exposure of the limits of Victorian/Edwardian patriarchal masculinity. The mythos, in one form or another, remains with us still, oppressing men and women. Men continue to attempt to perform the narrow range of possibilities provided by traditional masculinity. And perhaps some succeed. But the Great War revealed it as a damaged and damaging way of going on. I pray that a lasting legacy of the War might be that men are liberated from trying.

CHAPTER EIGHT

'A Battlefield' – How does 'The Land' hold the memory of war?

The Pilgrims at Luke Copse

'I was a dreamer ever…' – Ivor Gurney

Azure electric, an unbroken sky above Serre,
though a hint of cumulus, a curd summit
for the church's spire. We've come to measure

the distance between here and there, past and now,
from wood to village, time as study in geography –
days measured in inches, months in yards gained,

a decade in how long it took to plot the remains,
the ploughman surveys the field's annual harvest
of chalk and bone. *They buried them where they fell,*

the guidebook says, gravestones bring other news:
Lest we and *Greater Love, Nobly* and *Willingly,*
To the Memory, To the Glory and *Pace, Pace, Pace*

while Portland white bleeds green, the windward edge
enough to take bearings, discern the direction
of winter and storm, the yet to come.

Till then, sleepers, dream ever. It might be England,
a cornfield at Ampney Crucis as May turns gold,
the green shoot quickens to the swallows' dance.

About 800 yards west of the tiny village of Serre in Northern France is an attractive little wood. From the east edge of the trees chalky fields gently rise towards the village. A fit person could walk between wood and village in ten minutes, 'tops'. About fifty yards in front of that little copse of trees is a graveyard. Tiny, neat, it holds about three hundred graves. Look left from there and you see a series of graveyards stretching to the north. Look right and you see a series running towards the south. That quiet little wood is the Sheffield Memorial Park. It stands as memorial to the Pals battalions who fought and died on the first day of the Somme. In it is a memorial to the Accrington Pals and other Pals Battalions who – in 1914 – heard the call, joined up together and, ultimately, died together. It is, like so many places along the old Western Front in France, somewhere which, on the surface, communicates a sense of pastoral harmony and Nature's incorruptibility. However, as one steps into the wood one sees the after-effects of the years of shelling. The trees have grown up and over old shell holes.

The series of cemeteries I mentioned are a visual reminder of where the front line was on 1 July 1916 and of the desire on the part of the Imperial War Graves Commission to bury the lads where they fell. That little graveyard I mentioned is 'Queen's Cemetery.' A shattering reminder that so many of the lads who went over the top that morning got no more than a few yards. A little further back is Luke Copse Cemetery with 72 graves, mostly of Sheffield lads, who died in attacks there on 1 July and in November 1916. The village of Serre was one of the targets for the first morning of the Battle of the Somme, a mere 800 yards in front of the line. It was eventually taken in 1917 when the Germans withdrew from the site to stronger fortifications.

About two miles south-west of Serre is the village of Beaumont-Hamel. At 7.20 am, on 1 July 1916 just east of the village the British detonated an enormous mine at Hawthorne Ridge. The explosion was captured by the filmmaker Geoffrey Malins from a sunken road. The enormous explosion sent tons of earth, rock, along with God knows how many men into the air and Malins' film of it remains one of the most iconic visual records of the war, made all the more haunting by its silence. German units were simply vaporised. The road was about half-way into no-man's-land, accessed by a shallow tunnel. Along it units of the 1st Battalion, Lancashire Fusiliers had gathered for the 7.30am attack. Malins' film of the Somme includes footage of soldiers sat in the sunken road preparing to attack. They seem full of spirit and hope. As the whistle went the Fusiliers rose up and advanced on the German strongpoint. Practically none of the soldiers got more than a few yards. By lunchtime it was simply a refuge for the wounded. By evening, the battalion had lost 163 men killed, 312 wounded and 11 missing, almost half its number.

I could continue with example after example of battle sites for the length of a book. Part of the incommensurate nature of the Great War lies not simply in the scale of the slaughter and destruction, but in how every small detail holds the completeness of tragedy. When I visited the sunken road battle site in April 2016 I was struck by its tininess and ordinariness. It is simply an access road to a field. If it had not been for the large memorial to the 1/8 Argyll and Sutherland Highlanders at its entrance[1] one might have mistaken it for any other large rural track. And in many ways that's the point. It simply is a rural track that – without the constant rehearsal of memory – would sink back into ancient rhythms of rural life. Because that's what the Land does. It makes and remakes itself in and through the wounds we inflict upon it. As Sebastian Faulks indicates in his foreword to an anniversary edition of *Birdsong*, he chose the title of his striking Great War novel 'to suggest the indifference of the natural world to the human – human, as Philip Roth has put it, in the worst sense.'[2] This part of northern France has been fought over and refought over for centuries. The farmers depart and the farmers return to shape the land to an ancient formula.

Memory and memorialisation is always predicated on rehearsal. Our history as the literary species has been constructed through the rehearsal of that which we mark as significant. From cave drawings through the bardic singers of Greece and on to the written records we call 'history' we are makers of repetitions. If the Great War was at one level fought to be remembered then it is hardly surprising that we continue to re-inscribe it through visits to the battlefields and rituals of remembrance. One of the striking features of my recent visit to Picardy and Ypres was how, halfway up that sunken road the Lancashire Fusiliers had sheltered in, people had dug remembrance crosses into the bank. One had a faded message to a relative who had died there. The land works to remove the tokens of memory, but we resist. I travelled to the old front line in search of my grandfathers and was, of course, never going to find them. I went in search of the War, and a picture of England lost on the banks of Ancre, a picture that probably never was. If they were there at all they were there as symbols and tokens and tattered markers with names scribbled on them.

What do we walk when we walk the battlefields of France and Belgium? I can only begin to answer that by placing it in the context of other battlefield sites I've walked in the UK, like Towton in North Yorkshire. The late poet Geoffrey Hill, writing of Towton in 'Funeral Music', says 'A field/After battle utters its own sound/ Which is like nothing on earth, but is earth.'[3] Towton was the most horrifying battle of the War of the Roses and has famously been called the largest and bloodiest battle ever fought on English soil. It was reputed to have over 50,000 combatants and, after a bitter day of fighting in the snow on Palm Sunday 1461, left 28,000 dead. If that is in any way accurate (and the figures are disputed), it was an absolute catastrophe.

Hill's claims construct an irresistible truth. At the level of human pain, one needs little imagination to hear the after-effects of battle: the groans and moans of the dying or the flutter of banners, the creak of armour or a thousand other peculiar sounds of death and destruction. Yet, Hill's bleak lyric implies something more. That earth is changed in battle and sings or speaks in a manner which is incommensurate with earth that has not seen such violence. When I visited and walked the field of Towton on an utterly bleak day in March several years ago I was mindful of Hill's words. It was a few days away from Palm Sunday and there was sleet in the air. The battlefield itself is intersected by a small road and there is very little traffic. It was eerie and not impossible to believe that the earth itself had somehow been altered for good by what had happened there over five hundred years before. A clay pigeon shoot was taking place on the edge of the site. The wide open spaces of the moor only made the sound of the guns more disconcerting. It offered a strange reminder of modern violence on an ancient battle site.

Yet, if there is a case for claiming that earth that has been the site of serial violence is different, it is memory and narrative that produces the potent effects of the Great War sites. Towton might be a battle at which some people – most probably people from the old nobility and upper classes – might claim a kind of ancestral memory. It was, after all, a disaster for the Lancastrian nobility. The locals around Towton might also have a few folk-memory stories to tell. But the battle happened in an era when ordinary people didn't make the rolls of honour.[4] Towton constructs a catastrophe that shocks in terms of sheer numbers of deaths. Its isolated lonely location can generate odd effects, but its narrative does not speak through us. By contrast, to walk from Thiepval Wood up to the Ulster Memorial Tower, erected on the site of the infamous Schwaben Redoubt produces different effects. The Redoubt was the German strongpoint towards which the 36th Ulster Division charged on 1 July 1916 and to head up towards it is to traverse land both healed from and still utterly marked by death. The fields along which the German front line stretched are absolutely just fields now. And yet when they are ploughed in spring even an untrained eye can see the geometry of the trenches in the way the chalk is thrown up. The earth both here and especially around Ypres continues to not only give up the dead, but ordnance and other *matériel* of war.

So is it simply a matter of time that is at stake? As if the difference between a Somme or Passchendaele and a Towton is just a matter of centuries. Clearly it is a factor. All sinks away over time and one hundred years after a war is, after all, not such a long period. Yet such was the Great War's scale and such was the relative 'stasis' of the front for years at a time that millions of family histories have been altered forever along that fixed point – the Line. Yes, the Great War was a global conflict and it was fought not only on land but by sea and (for the first time) by air. But for the British – outside of a few months in 1914 and 1918 – it was essentially a war of concentration and stasis. Yes, troops were wheeled in and out of the Line, but the Line was the ultimate fact for years at a time. The sector around Ypres – which the British held for almost four years – was simply sown with blood. This was not the mobile war of the later twentieth century nor the set-piece war of the early nineteenth and previous centuries. Narrow front-line sections of France and Belgium simply swallowed the flesh of our ancestors – British, French, German and so on – for years. Wilfred Owen's 'Strange Meeting' captures the sense – gestured at by many war-weary soldiers – that the war was ancient, endless and fought over the same hellish space forever: 'It seemed that out of battle I escaped/Down some profound dull tunnel, long since scooped/Through granites which titanic wars had groined.'

This brings me to arguably the greatest (certainly most ambitious) poem of the Great War: David Jones' *In Parenthesis*.[5] Published in 1937, it's a startling, disconcerting Modernist achievement, lauded by Eliot and Yeats, and seen by the likes of Umberto Eco not so much as a poem, but a deconstructed novel-text. It follows the 'adventures' of Private John Ball (an echo of John Bull) in an Anglo-Welsh regiment from embarkation through to battle at Mametz Wood on the Somme. Epic in nature, it constructs a Modernist Homer, weaving Ball's experiences through myth, religion and Shakespearean and classical drama. As Fussell claims, '*In Parenthesis* poses for itself the problem of re-attaching traditional meanings to the unprecedented actualities of the war.'[6] That Ball finds himself in a Welsh–English regiment is indicative of the way in which the poem 'falls between' easy categories. If elements of the work are prose-like, asking questions of form and meaning, then the dual 'nationality' of the regiment prevents the 'narrative' from relying on the national myths of any one nation. The War happens 'in parenthesis'. The poem takes its questions of soldiers' motivations and the purpose of war into mythic space.

Ball encounters among others, Dai Greatcoat, the archetypical soldier. He has fought in all wars and in none. He was there when Cain killed Abel, he made 'a shithouse for Artaxerxes', he was at the gates of Troy and with Arthur at the Battle of Badon Hill. In essence, he boasts he cannot die and says, 'I was in Michael's trench when bright Lucifer bulged his primal Salient out' and suggests that War's genesis lies in this mythic cause: 'That caused it. That upset the joycart.' He invites Ball and the reader, as questors after the Grail of Meaning, to ask questions of the value of life and war. He concludes his great 'Warrior's Boast': 'You ought to ask, why? Why is this? What's the meaning of this?' For as Greatcoat makes clear, war has always been with us – from the mythic violence of the Bible, of Greece, of Wales and every nation, through to the present day. And if war is inscribed in the structure of living we cannot claim that it simply voids meaning or *is* the absence of meaning. Not quite. It is part of our human economy. Greatcoat concludes, 'Because you don't ask,/although the spear-shaft/drips,/there's neither steading – not a roof tree./I am the Single Horn thrusting/by night-stream margin/in Helyon.' It is as if our unwillingness to interrogate the meaning and place of war in the run of human affairs leaves the eternal soldier prosecuting the fight, caught up in the midst, and unable to get purchase on peace enough to understand his own fate.

Greatcoat indicates perhaps the key fissure in this book: what is the place and value of 'War', and the Great War in particular, in human affairs? And how am I (or anyone else) to make a reckoning with it in terms of my/one's family's participation in it? Jones' great poem makes a case for war as part of a tradition. The way it claims Biblical, classical and mythic references indicates its desire to align itself with a history of violence that nonetheless cannot erase meaning. In the midst of Flood, or filial murder or the serial wars of a text like the Bible, a thread of human value cannot be utterly destroyed. The Biblical text is a work of 'wrestling.' It is the story of Jacob and the Angel writ large. We – like Jacob – struggle in the midst of violence in the hope of blessing. The Bible – as a series of human interrogations of God and vice versa – wrestles with whether the Divine, as ultimate locus of meaning, delivers hope in the midst of and sometimes through violence. And, so, for example, by the end of the Book of Exodus, the Egyptian firstborn sons lie dead and a new Covenant is asserted. Destruction is wrought and a New Story begins. It is a structure which repeats itself in myriad forms throughout the text.

Yet, equally, I want to discount claims to war's significance and unavoidability. I want to write against it. I can adduce Christian and feminist reasons and yet what keeps calling me back is the fact of war and that men and women – some of whom I've known and loved – have participated in its ugly and extraordinary machinations. And I don't want to erase them and their experiences. Paul Fussell admires Jones' poetic achievement and yet points out that by placing war in its epic mode, *In Parenthesis* has 'no precedent for an understanding of war as a shambles and its participants as victims.'[7] But the risk of treating the Great War's participants as victims is that of treating them as just another statistic, which is another way of erasing their name or christening them with one global term: 'suffering'. Yes, Bert and Sam and countless others suffered as a result of the war, but I don't want them to be reduced merely to the position of 'victim'.

I want to conclude, as I think Jones does, that despite war's terror and its fracturing of the subject, meaning resides in the courage and faithfulness of the ordinary soldier. That even in the lice-ridden trenches *humans* lived. That there was, as Fussell claims about *In Parenthesis* itself, if not 'decency', then its possibility. Fussell says of the poem: '[it is] profoundly decent. When on his twenty-first birthday Mr Jenkins [the commander of Ball's platoon] receives both his promotion to full lieutenant and a nice parcel from Fortnum and Mason's, we are pleased. Details like these pull the poem in quite a different direction from that indicated by its insistent invocation of myth and ritual and romance. Details like these persuade us with all the power of art that the Western Front is not King Pellam's Land, that it will not be restored and made whole, ever, by the expiatory magic of the Grail. It is too human for that.'[8] I think we travel to the old front line still in search of the human. In search of Land that despite its fracturing and traumatisation retains the mark of human decency and the character of love.

One hundred plus years on, perhaps the likes of Owen and Jones would be most bewildered by the commodification of memory along the old front line. I certainly think Grandads Bert and Sam would be. For to walk certain sections of the front is to walk a carefully ordered souvenir trail. It is not necessarily tacky nor entertainment, but it has become commodified. That is, to go back to the Latin root of the term, the war has been made convenient and 'suitable' for visitors. It has become ordered and manageable for visits. Perhaps the central icon of this is Ypres itself. The town – with its extraordinary cloth hall, medieval cathedral and quaint central square and buildings – was essentially gutted by the war. For four years it was the deadliest place on earth. It is a testimony to the town burghers and determination of the Belgian authorities and allies that when one visits it now – at one level – one might barely know that war happened here. The Cloth Hall itself – once a profound statement of secular power in northern Europe and an architectural challenge to the greatest cathedrals – has been remade brick-by-brick. Such is the attention to detail that the late extension to the building – eighteenth-century rather than medieval – has been copied and rebuilt.

And yet despite the friendliness of the locals and the relaxed European feel of the town, there is something disconcerting about this recreation of Ypres. It constantly risks being a simulation or, as Baudrillard might put it, a simulacrum. The space of Ypres feels hyper-real, that is, it sets a 'truth' or constructs a 'reality' which conceals or subverts the facts of its destruction, even as it exposes what it seeks to conceal. Indeed, the endless iconography of the war which is 'weaved' into the fabric of the town (the poppies incorporated into shop signs, the 'World War One Museum', the 'World War One Experience' Tours) foreground the fact that Ypres will never achieve escape velocity from the war. It has the hyper-real character of a theme park. The nightly service at the Menin Gate – in which wreaths are laid, two minute's silence are kept and so on – is something I've found profoundly moving. Yet the fact that it has essentially happened in some form for the best part of 100 years is symbolic of the way the Great War has been definitive for Ypres. It cannot escape the war and its performance.

I say this not to be rude. When I visited Ypres, Passchendaele and its surroundings I was, in some ways, more powerfully affected by it than the Somme. The Somme remains the acme of British military tragedy, but the events in and around Ypres which culminated in the Third Battle of Ypres aka Passchendaele in 1917 have come to determine how most British people 'see' the war. The Salient, as it was known, allowed the Germans to attack from three sides for almost the entire length of the war. British and Empire forces were endlessly cycled in and out of this small area of just a few miles and – unlike some other sections of the Line (including until July 1916, the Somme) – it was never quiet. This place became a butcher's yard because, strategically, the British couldn't afford to give it up. This was the place that – as a result of awful weather, destruction of the water-table and serial shelling – became synonymous with mud and pointlessness. This was the place of which my grandad Bert said, 'Passchendaele was the worst.' Millions of men from both sides fought a hot war across the space of half a dozen kilometres for four years.

This – of all of the places I've visited – is the one most changed by war. Despite the stunning work of recreation by the Belgian people, Ypres is a place which, to paraphrase Hill, 'utters its own sound/Which is like nothing on earth, but is earth.' No amount of souvenirs or war-themed cafés or strange middle-aged men dressing up as soldiers and driving around the Salient can conceal this. Indeed, they reveal it all the more. The earth around the town is deeply wounded. It reveals piles and piles of ordnance every year. As one travels about this flat, lonely land one sees the remains of weaponry in fields. The number of cemeteries is overwhelming. Further back, behind the lines at Poperinghe (where chaplain, Tubby Clayton, had his famous house for rest and recuperation) is that grim little square where they shot British deserters at dawn. Every street, every lane and every field has a story to tell. Simply everywhere was consumed in the conflagration. Sometimes, it seems, war is something the land does not recover from. It stands as instruction. And in order to come to some reckoning with that instruction, that is also a condemnation, we have to commodify. We have to make it suitable for our engagement with it.

As early as 1918 writers were conscious that the need to make the incommensurate 'manageable' was almost inevitable. The simple fact that bodies would not be repatriated would draw the grieving to the site of wounds. A need to *see* what had happened would be irresistible. Indeed, in 1919 alone it was estimated that 60,000 people – many grieving relatives – visited the old front line. Yet even before the War had ended, writers were alert to its future commodification. Philip Johnstone's 'High Wood' appeared in *The Nation* on 16 February 1918. Many people now believe that Johnstone was a pseudonym for John Stanley Purvis, an officer who fought at and was wounded on the Somme and who, after the war, took Anglican holy orders. 'High Wood' imagines a post-war tour of the Somme battle site in which eight thousand bodies are buried where they fell. The poem is a dramatic monologue in the voice of a tour guide. After introducing the site in classic holiday tour guide style ('Ladies and gentlemen, this is High Wood...'), the speaker draws the tourists' attention to key features: 'Observe the effect of the shell-fire in the trees ... here is wire; this trench/ ... twelve times changed hands.' Dark humour is generated by the guide's imaginary interlocutors: 'Madame, please,/You are requested kindly not to touch ... the Company's property/as Souvenirs; you'll find we have on sale/A large variety, all guaranteed'. Tourists are requested not to stray from the path or drop litter.

Johnstone is profoundly alert to the irony implied by a tour guide instructing visitors not to drop litter in a place that a few years before 'dropped' human bodies like rags. In a post-war urge for 'preservation', tourists are requested not step from the path lest the site be 'damaged'. 'Destruction' must be 'preserved'. The requirements of solemn, indeed 'holy', memory mean that the integrity of the site must be maintained. Johnstone's intent reflects the bitter and black humour of the soldier. Yet, if Johnstone's poem questions the 'commodifying' mind – suggesting that if 'Hell' cannot be comprehended, the civilian mind will do its damnedest to try – the commodification of 'violent space' that took place after the War is not necessarily as questionable or surprising as one might think. The trauma of the War needed to be addressed and categories of comprehension had to be found. For the most part these were found in classic ideas of commemoration as old as the cultures of Greece and Rome, cultures that an empire like Britain's drew much of its inspiration from. As Jay Winter argues, '[the] vigorous mining of eighteenth and nineteenth-century images and metaphors to accommodate expressions of mourning is one central reason why it is unacceptable to see the Great War as the moment when "modern memory" replaced something else, something timeworn and discredited...[i.e.] "tradition."'[9]

Yet, commemoration – the work of 'calling to mind' – also constructed new ways of representing identity. One only needs to visit either Newfoundland Park on the Somme or the Vimy Ridge Memorial near Arras to appreciate this. These sites – dedicated to the combatants of Newfoundland and Canada respectively – represent profound moments for the formation of national identity. On 1 July 1916 the Newfoundland Regiment attacked as part of the second wave. It suffered 90 per cent casualties. The Newfoundlanders were volunteers and – as a small community –

suffered deaths on a disproportionate scale. A proud community bought the site in 1921 and have preserved it in their memory. Equally, Vimy has a memorial to over 11,000 Canadians killed, all volunteers. These two sites also represent over 80 per cent of all the preserved trenches on the Western Front. At Vimy, trenches have been 'concreted in' to ensure their preservation and integrity. The process has ensured that imagination is unnecessary to picture the site of so much violence. It shows graphically how, at one point, the distance between the Canadian and the German lines was about thirty yards. And yet because of the way it deprives the imagination of its work, an encounter with the site of so much loss becomes bizarrely flat and emotionless. And unreal. There is – despite the knowledge that death was here – a sense of the theme park. Children can run along the firing bays of the trenches. But, perhaps, the need to make 'the impermanent' – a trench will always collapse in on itself unless regularly maintained – permanent is a reflection of nations like Canada emerging from the imperial constructions of empire.

Pilgrimages have no doubt existed for as long as humans have sought to make sense of the world around them and invested place and people with symbolic significance. The idea of travelling to a place of significance for moral, personal or spiritual renewal, healing or enlightenment is part of the structure of our Christian heritage, even in Protestant contexts. The *peregrini* or pilgrim – the stranger who seeks wisdom – is a classic of faith. It is perhaps hardly surprising that the language of pilgrimage attached itself to visits to the Great War sites. To what do we travel when we travel to the Somme and Ypres? And for what? Well, if one is honest, one has to accept the fact that one travels to commodified space. As much as any pilgrim in Chaucer, one collects the badges of pilgrimage. One can say 'I have been here' and 'I have witnessed the Relics' – the graves and the trenches. One lays a wreath or pushes a Poppy Cross into the turf. And as one travels deeper into the pilgrimage space, 'time' changes. The graveyards and the land slow the pilgrim down. And one enters a time of 'remembrance' structured around silences – two-minutes and otherwise – and one walks from grave to grave, reading inscriptions that claim 'eternity': 'known unto God', 'greater love hath no man', 'thy will be done'. And occasionally one is startled by inscriptions which step outside the standard narrative, as with the one placed on the grave of 2nd Lieutenant Arthur Conway Young by his parents: 'Sacrificed to the folly that war can end war'. And one feels (or one doesn't) the expected emotions: gratitude, anger, sadness, etc. And one asks – as Dai Greatcoat the eternal soldier demands – 'Why? What was it for and what good did it bring?'

And if pilgrimage is about transformation – healing, reformation, resurrection – it is in the return 'home' that one notes what has changed. As I travelled home from my recent pilgrimage I noticed one effect above all others. As we drove back up through the Home Counties and the Shires I stared out of the window at fields of green wheat and yellow rape. And I kept expecting to see small cemeteries in the middle of fields. I half-saw the little green Commonwealth War Grave Commission signs up side streets in sleepy villages and grim towns. My way of seeing had been altered; I expected the marks of violence to be laid in ordinary places. For if being a pilgrim to France and Belgium has revealed anything – or in the least restated it – violence is appallingly ordinary. It marks all places. It is part of the structure of what we do and we do not know how to stop it, except perhaps in visions of the Christ or God. It happens anywhere, no matter how beautiful. We travel forward and we travel back and it is there. In the fields and hills of my grandparents' beloved Worcestershire. Among the limestone of the Cotswolds and the austere back-to-backs of Accrington. We catch it out of the corners of our eye. And it taunts us. And sometimes we dare to look back into its joyless, spiteful gaze and see if we can spot something more than despair and death.

CHAPTER NINE

'Poppies, Silence and The Broken Word' – Was language and symbol the ultimate casualty of the War?

Language is broken and 'there is a famine in the land'.[1] So suggests Barbara Brown Taylor, who goes on to claim that language has, as she puts it, 'taken a terrible hit'[2] from various quarters. Firstly, she notes that there is the assault of consumerism which 'forces words to make promises they cannot keep'. Words are chosen for their seductiveness rather than their truthfulness. We buy 'pods' for our coffee machines that claim that the coffee is 'freshly' roasted and ground, yet the pods can lie around on supermarket shelves for months. Secondly, she suggests that the news media's relentless desire for 'news' is corrosive; words have no longevity. Today's words are tomorrow's rubbish. With the advent of 24-hour news channels and social media, the turnover of information has become relentless. Brown Taylor suggests that the sheer proliferation of language acts as a prophylactic against meaning. Our care for words has decreased as words have proliferated. Our smartphones and tablets have made many of us endlessly distracted. We 'amuse' ourselves by constantly jumping between websites, social media sites and games. We want amusement rather than meaning.

We are assaulted by language. The noise of word and sound has made many of us hard of hearing. We do not listen well. George Steiner suggests that we are living in the aftermath of the broken covenant between the word and the world. Modern people's 'ears have been assaulted. They are fired upon every day by words intended to influence them, to manipulate them, to separate them from their cash.'[3] Speaking specifically about preaching (but perhaps about any speech-act) Brown Taylor claims, 'The problem is that nourishing words are so hard to find – words with no razor blades in them, words with no chemical additives.'[4] Her words hold good for the rest of our common and private lives. At the heart of the problem lies famine. 'Perhaps there is no proof that a famine exists except for the fact that people are hungry. Our problem is not too few rations, but too many.'[5] Words become dust in our mouths. They have no nourishment. We pile word on word and still we are not satisfied. 'The proof that we are in the midst of a famine of the Word are the suffocating piles of our own dead words that rise up around us on every side.'[6]

I am intrigued by the profusion of military metaphors in Brown Taylor's text – from talk of assault through to rations and, finally the striking image of 'the suffocating piles of our own dead words'. Knowingly or unknowingly she walks through the impact craters of the Great War, craters not insignificant to claims regarding the broken covenant between word and world. Nowhere is this clearer than in the corroded language of horror and futility used when people try to 'speak' the War. 'Any book about the war, or commentary on the literature or art it produced, will stress its horror … before we have even settled down to read the first stanza of Owen's "Dulce et Decorum Est", we are already murmuring to ourselves the old mantra, "the horror of war."'[7] Geoff Dyer's point is not to deny the nastiness of war, but to recognise that the language we use has descended into cliché; the language is eroded, as eroded perhaps as the old notions of 'glory' and 'honour'. Just as the language of consumerism, which Brown Taylor comments on, has become self-erasing ('New Improved Persil' means 'Same Old

Persil'), so has the language of horror. 'The words have bleached themselves out.'[8] Dyer quotes *The Times Educational Supplement's* review of Lyn Macdonald's *1914–1918*, and how it stresses 'the sickening repetitive monotony of hopeless horror'. Similarly, Nigel Vincy, in *Images of Wartime*, finds himself talking about the 'infinite horror' of the war. We live in an age of 'adjective inflation'. The simple formulae no longer seem to do their work. Language is 'consumed' – has become the final conquest of our consumerism – and it cannot feed us.

Perhaps Elaine Scarry's understated formulation – 'the main purpose and outcome of war is injuring'[9] – offers the best our uncertain language can give. It is a massive statement about war – so massive we miss its import. As she indicates one may scour many a military history without once finding an acknowledgement 'that the purpose of the event described is to alter (to burn, to blast, to shell, to cut) human tissue, as well as to alter the surface, shape, and deep entirety of the objects that human beings recognise as extensions of themselves.'[10] Indeed, Scarry outlines and details the paths by which the structure of war as injuring disappears from view. Crucially one of our strategies of denial focuses on language's capacity to conceal. The actions of injuring are renamed and re-described. Ordnance devices get called things like 'Cherrypicker' and campaigns are designated 'Goodwood' or 'Market Garden'. The day on which 35,000 Russians and 30,000 Germans lost their lives during the Great War's Battle of Tannenberg came to be known as The Day of Harvesting. As Scarry signals, these pastoral and flora-based terms act as gestures towards the notion of injury – for vegetation can be damaged – but hide the notion of pain. For plants are presumed to feel no pain.

People – like me – who have become fascinated by the events between 1914 and 1918 are inclined to invest them with elegiac mystery by calling them 'The Great War'. Of course, at one level, this is simply to adopt the term which arose after the war – 'The Great War for Civilisation'. To speak of 'Great War' is simply to co-opt an earlier designation. And yet from the outset the words were a prophylactic. Their re-description of four years of injuring and abuse is an act of investiture, like a man who has done remarkable, yet terrible deeds being made a knight. Those charged with prosecuting the war – politicians, soldiers, and so on – sought to act for the good, yet the consequences of their actions were beyond comprehension. They are too vast and also too dreadful. The term 'Great War for Civilisation' arose as both an act of propaganda – that is, as an attempt to invest the terrible with sense – as well as an elegant and elegiac rhetorical flourish whose ambiguity gestures towards the truth. The Great War, if one treats it as a single homogeneous 'creation', was *great* in the sense of being vast and huge and larger than any other previous conflict. It appeals to that cast of mind which thrills to the notion of size – the titanic and cosmic – yet this disposition easily shades into admiration. How easy for something massive to be recast as great in another sense, as terrific and brilliant.[11] The truth of war's injuring is elided by words. The name 'Great War' is both an act of covering up but also an attempt to redeem the seemingly irredeemable.

Whatever one might feel about claims regarding broken covenants between 'Word' and 'World', surely language was re-made by the Great War. For it effectively made absurd certain literary forms prevalent up to and including the War. For example, as Paul Fussell indicates, two days before the declaration of war the following appeared in *The Times*: '*PAULINE – Alas, it cannot be. But I will dash into the great venture with all that pride and spirit an ancient race has given me…*' The language as Paul Fussell argues, is 'that which two generations of readers had been accustomed to associate with the quiet action of personal control and Christian self-abnegation ("sacrifice") as well as with more violent actions of aggression and defense.'[12] This is the language of Robert Bridges, of Tennyson in Arthurian mood, of William Morris. It is the language of honour, glory and courage. It is a 'raised', essentially feudal language which, for the sake of shorthand, can be called 'high diction'. In this form of diction, 'friendship' becomes 'fellowship', 'danger' becomes 'peril', 'warfare' is 'strife', 'the sky' is 'the heavens', 'actions' are 'deeds' and so on. There is a kind of innocence expressed here, of which the 'prophylaxis of language' is equally indicative: words which after the war would constitute obvious *double entendres* (e.g. intercourse, ejaculation, etc.) could be used with confidence. The official order transmitted from British headquarters to the armies at 6.50 on the morning of 11 November 1918, warned that there 'will be no intercourse of any description with the enemy'. This language would be inconceivable in 1945. High diction, as common cultural coin, surely died in Flanders and Picardy.

Out of the death of high diction emerged T.S. Eliot's Modernist world with its rats' alleys, dull canals, and dead men who have lost their bones: it would take four years of trench warfare to bring these to consciousness. Ours is a time so beyond innocence, so instructed by cynicism and suspicion that it is hard not to condescend at news such as that which appeared in *The Times* of 9 August 1914:

At an inquest on the body of Arthur Sydney Evelyn Annesley, aged 49, formerly a captain in the Rifle Brigade, who committed suicide by flinging himself under a heavy van at Pimlico, the Coroner stated that worry caused by the feeling that he was not going to be accepted for service led him to take his life.

Fussell claims that, 'out of the world of summer, 1914, marched a unique generation. It believed in Progress and Art and in no way doubted the benignity even of technology'.[13] One is inclined to suggest that he overstates his case. Try telling a group of working-class cotton workers or miners that technology was benign and wasn't likely to kill you and they'd laugh. Fussell betrays his class-perspective. However, he has a point when he claims, 'The word *machine* was not yet invariably coupled with the word *gun*.'[14] Eleven years after the war Hemingway declared in *A Farewell to Arms* that 'abstract words such as glory, honor, courage, or hallow were obscene besides the concrete names of villages, the number of roads, the names of rivers, the numbers of regiments and the dates.' In the summer of 1914 few would have understood what on earth he was talking about. The Great War was not a full stop. But it was surely the end of one kind of story about history – the Meliorist fantasy that imagined a comfortable flow of events, grounded in progress from the past to the future.

Before the Great War there was an extraordinary prophylaxis of public speech and language. It seems clear that the war unearthed and enabled new ways of talking about war and violence. The question is whether the new linguistic forms and models simply offer – in the terms of someone like Scarry – new acts of obscuring. The literature of disillusionment represented by Sassoon, Graves, *et al.* was for the most part, I sense, just that. For ultimately the new ways of talking about the war which emerged were attempts to process the incomprehensible and incommensurate. Finding words for going on is one of our fundamental human activities. Poetry is one species of that endeavour and (depending on one's theoretical commitments) wants to mediate/express/construct Transcendence – which is another word for the incomprehensible, excessive and the terrible – and bring us into a new relationship with it. The words both make available and shape new worlds.

Ezra Pound's *Hugh Selwyn Mauberley* is an astonishing contribution to the literature of disillusionment. Pound did not serve in the War and the poem focuses on a poet whose life has become sterile and lost. Published in 1920 it not only provides some startling (unconscious) counterpoints to Owen's most famous poem 'Dulce Et Decorum Est' (At one point Pound says, 'Died some, pro patria,/Non "dulce" non "et decor".../Walked eye-deep in hell/Believing in old men's lies, then unbelieving/Came home to many deceits') but closes with a devastating assessment of the war:

> *There died a myriad,*
> *And of the best, among them,*

For an old bitch gone in the teeth,
For a botched civilisation,

Charm, smiling at the good mouth,
Quick eyes gone under earth's lid,

For two gross of broken statues,
For a few thousand battered books.

It is dazzling poetry which contextualises the war in a way which I suspect most combatants could barely dream of. The notion of dying for 'an old bitch gone in the teeth' retains visceral power, underlined by the sharp contrast with the stately, classical notion of 'quick eyes gone under earth's lid.' Pound's assessment of the war is starker when we place it alongside the authorised, standard picture of the war as 'The Great War for Civilisation'. Pound's conclusions indicate the fissure in life and culture, but if it extends our understanding and is grounded in the emerging Modernist move, it is already mythologising the war. It re-describes war and the war in culturally comprehensible terms.

Pound was no serving soldier. The likes of Rosenberg, Sassoon and Owen were. Rosenberg and Owen in particular were capable of the most startling images. They draw close to a linguistic exposure of war as injuring. In 'Dead Man's Dump', Rosenberg describes a cart moving over a pile of dead men: 'The wheels lurched over sprawling dead/But pained them not, though their bones crunched.' Later in the same poem he talks of 'A man's brains splattered on/A stretcher-bearer's face.' In 'Dulce Et Decorum Est', Owen provides some of the defining mythic images of not only the Great War but of War itself: 'Bent double, like old beggars under sacks/knock-kneed, coughing like hags, we cursed through sludge.' His description of the gas victim still resonates: 'His hanging face, like a devil's sick of sin;/If you could hear, at every jolt, the blood/Come gargling from the froth-corrupted lungs,/ Obscene as cancer.'

Rosenberg is significant for a number of reasons. Not least, he of all the 'War Poets' represents the position of the ordinary soldier. His voice almost speaks for the silence of my grandfathers. For Rosenberg was an outsider. He was Jewish and working-class, and had not received even a grammar-school education. He was a misfit even in the new Citizens' Army. He was assigned to a Bantam battalion because he didn't reach the expected height of 5' 3" and suffered from ill-health throughout his time in the Army. His lack of formal education in the classics of poetry arguably gave his raw talent and painterly eye (he was also a gifted artist) space to play boldly with traditional poetic form. His best work remains extraordinary. 'Break of Day in the Trenches', for example, anticipates David Jones' use of mythic tropes ('The darkness crumbles away./It is the same old Druid Time as ever') by decades. However, its sense of the vile particularity of trench life ('Only a live thing leaps my hand,/A queer sardonic rat') is intense and concentrated. Paul Fussell's claim that this poem is the greatest of the War has genuine traction.

However, we should not try to make of Owen and Rosenberg's poetry what it is not. Owen's own assessment of the import of his work – that it is about the pity of war – is revealing. He is not trying to write War, for perhaps it is unwritable. The very fact that Owen has become – along with other poets of disillusionment – the conventional expression of how we see war is the signal for that. A twelve-year-old doing a poetry exercise can layer up worn-out metaphors on the futility of war as laboriously as sandbags being lifted to reinforce a parapet. It is also noticeable how far even the likes of Rosenberg and Owen work with traditional and established poetic and linguistic forms – notably elegy. Fussell also indicates how Owen's writing has a strong homo-erotic turn connecting it with 'the tradition of Symonds, Wilde, Rolfe, Charles Edward Sayle, John Francis Bloxham, and other writers of warm religio-erotic celebrations of boy-saints, choirboys, acolytes and "server-lads."'[15] If the war poets make traditional martial verse absurd, they are no Modernists. Perhaps it is someone like e.e. cummings who draws closer to the linguistic breakdown, the fundamental injuring that is effected by war. The terseness and oddness of his syntax is both precise and odd:

> *the bigness of cannon*
> *is skilful,*
>
> *but i have seen*
> *death's clever enormous voice*
> *which hides in a fragility*
> *of poppies...*
>
> *i say that sometimes*
> *on these long talkative animals*
> *are laid fists of huger silence*
>
> *I have seen all the silence*
> *filled with vivid noiseless boys*

Metaphors died and metaphors rose in the Great War. The idea of war as game and adventure died. Reality could no longer sustain them, if they ever had. New images and symbols arose, not least the Flanders' Poppy. It can seem extraordinary to us now that the poppy was ever other than a symbol of memory and remembrance. Yet, rosemary has a deeper and better claim. In myth it was held to improve memory and its use in funerals and commemorations is ancient. In *Hamlet* Act IV, scene 5, Ophelia says, 'There's rosemary, that's for remembrance.' For ANZAC Day, rosemary is worn for the Aussie and New Zealand troops who fought at Gallipoli, where a famous strain of rosemary grew in abundance.

In John McCrae's famous (if not terribly well-written) poem, 'In Flanders Fields', '...the poppies blow/Between the crosses row on row.' As a result of the churning up of the land, poppy seeds were widely spread and grew quickly and easily in the broken stretches of no-man's-land. It is moot how far veterans felt the Haig Fund's post-war use of the ubiquitous poppy image was an offence to their experiences. As a teenager in the 1980s I remember how – in an act of violent solidarity with perceived injustices against 'Tommy Atkins' and the militarism of past and present leaders – we'd try and file off Haig's name from the remembrance poppies we wore. What is clear is that comprehensible as the use of the poppy image is, it remains another means of covering up, of making more manageable, the reality of war. Of course, all metaphors and ways of expression reveal as much as conceal. We cannot avoid them. We are myth-making creatures. My fear is that in creating myths about war we, *de facto*, create transcendent justifications for its precise and brutal acts of injuring and damaging.

Perhaps then the only response – the only way of trying to articulate war – is, ironically, silence. 'I have seen all the silence/ filled with vivid noiseless boys,' claims Cummings. Cummings' line is fascinating precisely because of its dreamlike quality. His syntax and expression take us outside normal time and space. The move from 'i' to 'I' in the poem is surely deliberate, but puzzling, as if the status of his subjectivity is in question. Equally, what does it mean to see the silence? Some of the accounts of 'shell-shock', in which the living see their dead comrades coming towards them in dreams, have this odd troubling character. They are part of a culture of dreaming which connects the twentieth century with classical images of dreams found in Homer and other places, in which the dead come to accuse or guide or direct. His noiseless boys may be vivid because they are dead and covered in blood, but they might equally be characters in a vivid dream. Dreams have, since the dawn of culture, been seen as the meeting place between the dead and the living, our ancestors and us. As E.R. Dodds puts it, 'the dream world offers the chance of intercourse, however fugitive, with our distant friends, our dead, and our gods.'[16] One dimension of silence is the muteness of the sacrificial victim. Yet, as with the dead coming towards us in dreams, sometimes their muteness is also accusation.

Scarry suggests that war has structural connections with torture. Both are about injuring. The fundamental character of torture – as explored by the likes of Wisnewski and Emerick[17] – is the injuring (and destruction) of 'the self' by the use of subjectivity against itself. Physical and emotional torture rests upon the subject becoming an object. It relies upon the fact that – via pain – the subject of torture can no longer rely upon his or her body. It becomes the subject's own enemy and only the one inflicting the torture holds the power of ending the injuring. Part of the injuring and cruelty of torture is how it makes the victim's own body/identity their enemy and forces them to transfer their faith and hope to the perpetrator. For only the perpetrator has the means to end the tortured one's pain. The victim's subjectivity is destroyed and therefore silenced. It is striking how easy it is – precisely because it is a supra-national activity – to miss this dimension of war. The fundamental truth of its prosecution – its place in our politics as it were – is that it's about turning men into silent flesh/meat. I am not talking about the command structure of war, as such, but the fact of injuring and killing. That even as we become ever more insulated from war's 'facts' by technology – by what Baudrillard gestures towards in the notion of hyper-reality – war is about taking subjects 'out'. Its aim is to make them useless objects – dead flesh. Silent meat

Here is a point at which Christianity has striking theological insights to offer. For at the heart of its central narrative is a work of torture – the Cross – and a critique of the idols our culture makes for itself. At its simplest (and therefore its most elusive), 'The Cross' signals that violence is not the final word; it is not the quiddity of the World. Insofar as 'violence', torture, etc. makes that claim it is a simulacrum of reality. It is idolatrous. The 'Easter Event' – Resurrection and Cross, in concert – signals that though 'The World' appears to have the structure of annihilation (of body, of love and so on), the Living God takes death into herself and is not destroyed. And in the Garden on that first Easter Day, the

Risen God's offering is not revenge or the promise of annihilation; she offers peace and reconciliation and a new beginning. She comes offering the hush of silence rather than shouts of anger. A silence that is peace rather than the silencing characteristic of regimes which propagate violation and death.

There are other horizons of silence, of course, not least civic or community silence. We cannot capture now how complete the silence on Armistice Day would have been between the wars, especially in the immediate post-war era. By the 1980s I think many of us had expected the practice to begin dying out, left to a few civic expressions each Remembrance Sunday. However, as the Great War generation began to disappear there seemed to be an upsurge of interest in keeping the silence. The news began to report how not only on Remembrance Sunday but also on Armistice Day people were keeping silence. Britain's ongoing adventuring in world affairs – and the consequent regular deaths of soldiers – has no doubt been a factor in this sustained phenomenon. The upsurge of interest in finding one's family past – encouraged by ready access to historical records via the internet – has also ensured that more people are aware of their family's connections to the great struggles of the twentieth century. But perhaps also the communal nature of the silence has become a kind of matins for a culture uncertain of what it shares and of where it is going.

If it is important to bring a hermeneutics of suspicion to state-legitimised practices of silence – for surely the powerful can use it for their own ends – it is also important to recognise that some kinds of silence might nonetheless be an appropriate response to violence. It has become fashionable in a number of situations – upon the death of an admirable person in sport, for example – to offer a minute's applause instead of a minute's or two minutes' silence. Silence is perceived as too solemn, as lacking that key dimension of modern living – the celebration of a life. It is striking how modern funerals have assumed the character of celebrations and memorials. The rigorous bleakness of the Book of Common Prayer is too spartan for us. The way silence exposes us to ourselves is too much for us. In the context of mourning and death 'silence' signifies the reality we shall all face – that we too are ultimately dust. It is what will greet us all one day.

Jay Winter[18] persuasively argues that the rituals of remembrance which emerged around the time of the Great War represent more of a testing of traditional civic and religious concepts than some sort of radical break with the past. This is certainly a helpful corrective when many of us are inclined to emphasise the profound rupturing impact of the violence. The use of silence and flowers (poppies) and the singing of hymns around a focal point (a memorial, rather than the Eucharistic table) are contiguous with traditional Christian practices. The language of sacrifice, of dying that others might live and so on was a co-option and extension of common notions. And it is not clear what else a grieving culture could do. To attempt to face the scale of injuring made by four years of fighting without some gesture towards a transcendent meaning would surely have broken the nation.

Yet if a kind of active, attentive silence is one appropriate response to the war's project of silencing, it cannot be enough. For if the Great War has defined our responses to war in many ways and has done so by co-opting Christian symbols and practices, the civic rituals fail to take those Christian practices seriously enough. The Christian story was complicit in the war in any number of ways, but it also draws as close to an honest apprehension of state-legitimated violence as any other strategy we have. For Christ is not so much about the glory of sacrifice as the exposure of violence and its mechanics, as well as the subsequent invitation to commit to a different way. For the God in Christ is all about passion: he becomes our victim, handed over to us, the subject of our jealousies, fears and our desire to be in control. This is a god tortured at the end of a whip. This is a god who is mocked and killed. This is a man thoroughly caught up in and destroyed by the violence of the world.

In this ironic world it is the perpetrators of violence who claim to be agents of light: the keepers of the peace, the protectors of the faith and the saviours of the nation and civilisation. And on any human calculation these claims are reasonable: to wish to protect the nation from further violence or from one's occupiers (or in the case of war, from an outside threat) is humanly commendable. These are good causes. These are people standing up for something more than personal self-interest – they seek to save the nation. These people, then, are wearing metaphorical white hats. Yet, the only kind of god who wants or needs a blood offering is us. The bloodthirsty god whose hunger is only appeased by the death of his only son haunts our imaginations. It is the kind of image that can keep us as frightened children; keeping us in bondage instead of liberating us.

The oddness of Jesus – his revelatory power in relation to war and violence as injuring – lies in his full humanity. The philosopher Stanley Cavell's study of *King Lear* and his remarks about the character of Cordelia, in particular, help us appreciate this profound humanity of Christ. Cordelia has often been compared to Christ in the honest faithfulness of her commitment to love rather than flattery. She pays the price for refusing to flatter her father Lear: she is exiled. In the midst of Lear's later 'madness' she forgives him for banishing her. Edmund's perfidy – he hangs Cordelia – prevents Father and Daughter from truly consummating their reconciliation. Cavell suggests, 'If Cordelia resembles Christ, it is by having become fully human, by knowing her separateness, by knowing the deafness of miracles, by accepting the unacceptability of her love, and by nevertheless maintaining her love and the whole knowledge it brings.'[19] Christ is fully human for – in the end, in his injuring and torture, his pain and his death – he is forsaken and separate; he knows the deafness of miracles and yet maintains his love. He is the victim who transforms his fate into destiny and exposes our violence, accepts his annihilation and yet does not demand revenge.

If Christ embraces humanity he also represents God. This god embraces victimhood – silencing, objectification and injuring – and exposes what our violence does. He invites us to commit to another way. Resurrection is a symbol of this invitation. For this risen God is not one who glories in his sacrifice, nor comes seeking revenge. The invitation is to reconciliation. The offer is forgiveness. The challenge is to make a commitment to a Way of going on which rejects silencing, objectification and injuring. The Risen Christ leaves it up to us to make that commitment. He exposes what state violence is – with war being an example of that – and reveals how it is part of each of us. We can no more disown it than dare revel in it.

Yet, there is power in our attentive civic silence. If it always runs the risk of allowing us to forget the injuring at the heart of war for another year, it also gestures towards war's incommensurability. Other elements of the civic liturgy – the funereal music, the poppies – are clearly capable of multivalent meanings: as rituals *for* the living they seek to communicate that the dead have not died in vain, that war (and the Great War in particular) is not mere tragedy, but is redeemable. The rituals indicate that war holds within itself its own transcendent meaning. Yet without the ironic critical narrative of Christ – the narrative which both exposes the victim-making nature of civic/state power and invites us to commit to a community of atonement – these rituals run the risk of being endless, repetitive rehearsals that do not break out of patterns of injuring and abuse. They become icons of our incapacity to learn from the past, of our obsession with identical repetition. They ensure that we keep prosecuting war. In contrast, a community grounded in the practices of breaking bread and sharing wine, of rehearsing the story of Christ's humanity and divinity, knows the power of liturgy and ritual, of its repetition but knows it is not enough. The sharing of divine food, again and again, is never the same, for it is both about being fed for living but also about taking the victim and the redeemer into the self and then into the world. It is about movement. It is about being faithful to the Way.

I'm worried. My grandfathers' presence in this book is in danger of going missing for the sake of some fancy philosophising. Yet, I want to keep them present. For a little while longer. Sam the grandfather who I hardly knew; Bert the grandfather who hardly spoke. I'm not ready to let them go. I do not want them to be cause for fancy theorising. I want to keep and honour their particularity and say that what they did was not mere chaff or that they were dupes or just victims. That would just be another way to let them join the ranks of the forgotten or the missing. So I shall continue to keep the silence our culture has made for itself every Remembrance Sunday. And I shall try to be part of a community of atonement that keeps our violence in sight and tries to live another way. I shall try to live in the midst of compromise, a creature of unclean, but hopeful hands.

Postscript

'A few, a few, too few for drums or yells,
May creep back, silent, to village wells,
Up half-known roads...'
Wilfred Owen, 'The Send-Off'

Wilfred Owen's poem is powerful and evocative, belonging, like so much (well remembered) Great War literature to the genre David Stevenson calls 'elegiac pathos.'[1] Owen's closing claim is evocative, but, statistically, is wildly inaccurate. The British war dead (excluding the British Empire) were around three quarters of a million; by 1918, over four million men had seen service in the British army. To be hard-nosed about it, it simply wasn't the case that 'a few, too few' returned to 'sad shires'; overwhelmingly, it was most who returned. In brutal terms, 750,000 died, but over 3,500,000 returned, more or less intact. In 1919, demobilisation proceeded at the rate of 10,000 men a day for six months. And yet my dad tells a story which resonates sympathetically with Owen's sentiment. It is one of the few stories I've regularly heard my dad tell about his own father. Because of the rarity of his tales about his dad it makes me want to believe it more. The story my dad tells is of Sam's return at the end of the war.

Sam's return was to a Worcestershire apparently untouched by war – to Abberley and its clock tower, and its closed-in lanes untroubled by traffic, to an Abberley Hill as solid as it had been when, five centuries before, Henry IV had sat atop it and 'stared' at Owain Glyndwr on an opposing hill. A Worcestershire fixed by the slow moving Severn and lively Teme. A Worcestershire of green and brown turned-over fields – both similar to and (in that immediate post-war era) utterly different from Picardy, that land of the Ancre and the Somme. A Worcestershire, most of all, utterly different to the baked bleakness of Mesopotamia. I sometimes wonder if Sam shook his head momentarily as he walked down the half-remembered lanes towards home wondering whether he had been returned to France or was genuinely back in Blighty. Or whether he wondered whether he knew what home was anymore anyway. More likely he hurried home to his mother, just desperate for a cup of tea, perhaps an egg or two and then bed.

Finally, he saw it – the little cottage in a hook in the road, The Lodge, and his step quickened as he approached the front door, excited and terrified about coming home. And so Sam knocked the door and his mum answered. She opened the door and they looked at each other and his mum didn't recognise the man before her – this was just a lousy scarecrow of a man, his skin still itchy from lice, not the proud youth who'd marched away with a cheeky smile a few years before. Even the eyes had changed. She looked and looked at the raggedy man and was about to tell him to sling his hook, when he spoke, and of all things, his voice hadn't changed. Despite his adventures he'd kept his rich Worcestershire burr.

Well that's how the story goes anyway – almost a Worcestershire *Le Retour de Martin Guerre*. And at the level of myth, of story, it is every returning soldier's story – the story of the effects of war, of growing up under the shadow of the gun, of how everyone is changed by violence and journey. Of how nobody stays the same and no one can quite tell what is real anymore. Sam's physical appearance, of course, was a cosmetic matter. It was nothing a good bath, a few months' decent food and some civilian clothes wouldn't solve. But the deeper sadnesses and silences were not so easily solved, and ultimately when Sam married May, she bore the scars of that silence on her body for many years to come. There *were* 'sad shires', but not quite as Owen imagined them, and May's wounds were symptoms. And nothing would really be the same again. When these young 'heroes', like my own Grandad Sam, 'went on binges in local taverns, broke windows and chairs, assaulted girls (or in Sam's case my gran), or caused an incipient scandal, the invariable response of the citizenry was to hush up the outrage, to show 'tolerance'[2] and lenience.

Sam and Bert – and indeed Aunty Betty – fall outside the purview of so much that has been written about the war, or at least most of what has been written that has shaped reasonably well educated, middle-class opinion of the Great War. The perception that it was completely futile is persistent among the informed – a reflection of the impact of the literature of disillusionment upon many (including, until relatively recently, myself). Other factors are involved in this myth of the war – economic and political, as well as cultural – but the Great War is strikingly one which invites being read through literary categories. Even with a hard-nosed historian like David Stevenson, the temptation to read the War through literary categories seems overwhelming: 'contemporaries on both sides at once hated the slaughter and yet felt unable to disengage from it, embroiled in a tragedy in the classical sense of a conflict between right and right.'[3] Aeschylus would have approved. Sam and Bert's experience whilst shared in many respects with the officer-poets of the war (officer and private sharing life in common in ways barely conceivable pre-war) was, in truth, not captured by Sassoon's angry-elegiac reflections.

The literature of disillusionment only underlined my grandfathers' silence and marginalisation; it certainly didn't give voice to it. And yet there is one literary work which, unexpectedly, gives some voice to their silence – Joan Littlewood's *Oh! What a Lovely War*. That I say this may seem surprising. For, this rather arch, theatrical piece devised in the turbulent 1960s may seem even more removed from my grandfathers' experience than Sassoon's. In one sense this perception is absolutely correct. *Oh! What a Lovely War* is arch and, in almost too many ways to outline, deeply imbalanced.[4] I have seen the stage version of the musical – presented as a *Pierrot* show – and felt disconnected and deflated. It seemed too pleased with itself to do honour to the dead and the lost. In contrast, I found Attenborough's film version overwhelming. For instead of working with the *Pierrot* theme the action centres on the experience of an ordinary 'representative' family, the Smiths. Certainly, Attenborough's take is – for the most part – hardly subtle, yet its strange power lies in its focus on a family chewed up and destroyed by the War. All five of the male adults are killed or lost. The women are left behind. The conclusion of the film consists of a camera panning out from the dead members of the Smith family into an impossibly vast cross-filled cemetery. Jerome Kern's haunting tune 'They Didn't Believe Me' plays as the surviving members of the Smith family sit in the midst of the crosses. I cannot watch it without tears, the two simple verses of the song capturing myriad ironies of the War:

> *And when they ask us, how dangerous it was,*
> *Oh, we'll never tell them, no, we'll never tell them:*
> *We spent our pay in some café,*
> *And fought wild women night and day,*
> *'Twas the cushiest job we ever had.*

> *And when they ask us, and they're certainly going to ask us,*
> *The reason why we didn't win the Croix de Guerre,*
> *Oh, we'll never tell them, oh, we'll never tell them*
> *There was a front, but damned if we knew where.*

But if *Oh! What a Lovely War* is deeply theatrical and politically cack-handed, the reason it draws closest to the voices of my grandfathers, lies in its use of the Tommies' sometimes bawdy, often cynical, songs. These songs delve into a world far beyond 'A Long Way To Tipperary' or 'Pack Up Your Troubles'. The way soldiers subverted famous hymn tunes ('What A Friend We Have In Jesus/The Church's One Foundation' and so on) and other well-known music and phrases for their own cynical purposes takes us much closer to the grumbling, the anger and the courage of the ordinary fighting man than the poetry of Owen. 'Christmas Day in The Cookhouse' and 'If The Sergeant Steals Your Rum, Never Mind' contain that strain of bawdy, often blasphemous humour that has been the mark of the private soldier since – to indulge in a touch of classical elegy myself – the first bridgehead was founded on the shores of Troy. The British genius for grubby toilet humour and wordplay found brilliant expression in the bleak mechanisms of the trenches. No one can construct the voices of my grandfathers now. The silence is too great. But the nearest glimpses lie in the songs they would have marched to, would have whistled while on fatigues and sang with mates to get a bit of courage before the next attack. The songs help us find a way back to our forebears.

The voices of my grandfathers are lost forever. I cannot hope to reconstruct their thoughts, hopes and dreams. I suspect they approached life in that grim, hardy attitude that English yeomen have expressed since the early days of agriculture. Theirs was a suspicious, reserved world and, perhaps, with good reason – they fled the land in 1914 only to take their skills into the harsh geometry of the trenches. And upon their return agriculture greedily placed its yoke around them again. As young men who knew nothing different, Bert went back to ploughing and Sam returned to Witley Court, in charge of the horses. From the slow, straight furrows of his plough, Bert would feel, by turns, the windy bite and the heat of England on his neck and still he would press on. In my more romantic moments I imagine that some days, perhaps, maybe once every few years, as his mind quietly tried to make sense of his youth, he might have heard on the breeze the voices of dead comrades singing, 'Old soldiers never die, the young ones wish they would.' And then he'd smile, and stop, and finally move on, trying to forget all he wished he'd never learnt in France and Flanders.

~~~

I'm walking through Gheluvelt Park. The low February sun is unexpectedly warm and has surprised a handful of others away from their laptops or the TV or hurried shopping trips to pretend that spring is upon us. A man in a pac-a-mac tries and fails to keep pace with his eager spaniel; a couple of skater boys whisper conspiratorially about a pretty girl; a mother fusses over her pink daughter struggling on a pink bike. And I realise that from the moment I began writing about the War and my family I would have to come to this park. It has been waiting for me. This little park, just a few hundred yards square, was always going to be a place of reckoning. Wherever I've been over the past few months – to see my parents or my younger brother, plodding up the motorway between, driving around Manchester – I've been catching it out of the corner of my eye. It's a pressure in my veins building since I was eight years old.

I've arrived at the very centre of the park. Ahead of me is an ornamental pond. Mallards plough suspiciously through its shallow waters. The drakes already seem to be carving out their territories as if anxious for the mating season when they can enact again their brutal rituals on the ducks. The ducks perhaps sensing this, keep their distance. A moorhen thwacks its webbed feet on the muddy shore. And set in the very centre of this pond at the heart of the park is a bandstand, slate roofed, metal frame painted black and red, adrift from dry land without any obvious connection. What once may have been a footbridge juts out from grass and goes nowhere, as stupid as a branch snapped from a trunk. No brass band will be playing there today and the water birds don't seem displeased.

I think of my grandfathers. Of how they enacted the brutal rituals of soldiering in trenches no further away from their opponents than the length of this park, two hundred yards from end to end. And I think of the churning of wetlands, remembering Timothy Findlay's image of Flanders: 'The mud. There are no good similes. Mud must be a Flemish word. Mud was invented here … in 1916, it was said that you "waded to the front". Men and horses sank from sight … their graves, it seemed, just dug themselves and pulled them down.'[5] I think of my grandfathers, with Worcestershire grown in their flesh, seeing the countryside of France and Belgium churned to sludge; the land of their souls could never be pure again. And I'm so angry – angry at the brass plaques of commemoration at the entrance to the park telling us that the top brass of the war, Haig, Robertson and so on, paid their respects here; angry that this park was offered as a sanctification of sacrifice.

I think about the innocence of the bandstand, that fixture of our vision of Edwardian and Victorian England: women in enormous hats and elegant clothes, carrying parasols, men in high collared suits, the occasional red-uniformed soldier. This innocent bandstand absurdly stuck in the middle of a pond with no obvious connection to solid ground, a statement on the absurdity of the twentieth century. With each rivet of its construction, the makers were trying to re-capture the peace and hope of the pre-war age; the elegance of its construction only underlining what had been lost. And behind me the 449 road hums with people-carriers and heavy goods, the squeal of a moped. The silence of the park is being crowded out; with each year, its silence becomes fainter. But still I sense the silence of my grandfathers, growing fainter. It is as if they are joining the missing of Ypres, the Somme, of Gheluvelt and Neuve Chappelle. They are disappearing. They are letting me go.

I think about the concept of 'travelling back'. Of how we cannot 'go back' and yet how we try. I think about the countless times I've returned 'home' to the little village of Hartlebury. The place I grew up, and where so many of my family including Granny and Grandad Collins made their 'home'. And how there will come a point when I make the journey back there for a final time. No more to make that turn left under the Black Bridge, before I take the road right past the barn from which my younger brother sold endless varieties of potatoes in his first Saturday job as a youth. No more to head up over the brow of the hill to see the sandstone tower of St James' Church poking out from between the trees. A church at the centre of the village, but perhaps no longer at the centre of community. Where many members of my family, including me, were baptised. The site of family weddings and funerals. The beginning and end of so many family stories.

I think of how the time will come when I will make a final trip past Hartlebury First School, so tiny now, so huge to me once. The place where my mum began school, and my brothers and sister, and me, and my nephew Mike too. Heading on up Quarry Bank past the old Grammar School and the Big House and the houses we passed morning and evening as kids as we travelled down the Bank to school, kicking leaves in autumn, ploughing through snow in winter. I think of travelling back to my parents' cottage one last time. And, as I think about all this, I know that we shall not all be remembered. We have our time and *The wind goes over it and it is gone*. And that is ok. But, as I consider this, I want to say that at least for some of us – as ordinary, insignificant people – there is a staving off of that forgetting in the great act of remembrance each November. Time is held back. We say the ordinary people, not just the powerful, are worthy of remembrance too. And in a time of cultural amnesia is that such a sin?

I realise I'm weeping, but I don't think it's just for my grandparents. I don't think it's for the death of a shabby, but tantalising vision of an England that never was. It is for all the innocence that I've lost – or, if I'm honest, I imagine I've lost. I feel ashamed – after all these words, thinking and study, does it come down to that? My self-pity? Crying for a myth of me that never was. But still I mourn. Beside me the summer shrubs are pared back to skeletons; the pink girl struggles on in the distance. Somewhere a dog barks. And, in the brightly-coloured, plasticky children's area a boy plays on the swings, soaring higher and higher, momentum and gravity pushing him to ever greater heights. And as it hits its peak, he jumps out and forward, soaring, soaring. And he keeps on soaring.

NOTES

Introduction

1   One of the abiding questions about the Imperial Era in British life was the extent to which the default identity was English. Certainly it was not uncommon for English and British to be seen as interchangeable in some circles, especially the 'adventure fiction' genre represented by the likes of Childers, Buchan and Rider Haggard. Scottish, Welsh and Irish identity had to negotiate the complex dynamic between distinctiveness and absorption into a national collective. This complexity is indicated not only in the ongoing association of Englishness with post-imperial embarrassment, but by the fact that at the practical level the Scots, in particular, were huge players in the growth of Empire. Scottish soldiers also provided some of the elite troops in the Great War and were both feared and died in vast numbers. Scottish friends tell me that remembrance of their loss is marked by a different sentiment than in England – the remembrance is more likely to be united with anger at their death for an English empire and war.

2   At a time when the UK is reflecting again on its place in and relationship with 'Europe', one of the tropes that's in play, at least in some people's minds, is a 'dream of England'. It hardly needs pointing out that its use by racist and xenophobic groups is a reminder of how dangerous it can be to speak of 'England'.

3   Many, if not most, of these people were not part of the white, Christian social elite and their stories as people of colour and/or non-Christian faith have been erased from practices of memorialisation.

4   Richard Holmes, *War Walks: From Agincourt to Normandy* (London: BBC, 1996), 120.

5   Philip Jenkins, *The Great and Holy War: How World War 1 Changed Religion for Ever* (Oxford: Lion Hudson, 2014), 4–5.

Prologue

1   Though, as we've discovered since, both Bert and Sam's army records were among the 60% completely destroyed in the Blitz of 1940.

2   See Blythe's classic 1969 study *Akenfield: Portrait of an English Village* for a passionate and moving study of (Eastern-) English village life, some of whose inhabitants' experiences were shaped in and around the Great War.

3   For an utterly haunting reflection on the dissonance and connections between rural life and trench life listen to 'Home, Lad, Home' by folk duo Belshazzar's Feast on 2010 album, *Find the Lady*. As the song unfolds – in a trench in Flanders – a whole way of rural life seems to unpick itself.

4   When I found out that he'd been in the 'Labour Corps' I thought, 'as a pioneer maybe he wasn't that exposed to the fighting.' Then I discovered that this section of the army, which came into existence in the last section of the war, exposed men who – as a result of serious wounds were no longer quite fit for the front line – to potentially horrific conditions just behind (and sometimes in front of) the Front Line.

5   In particular, 'The Lads in their Hundreds', captures both a pre-war pastoral, yet seems to foreshadow the War. The text is ostensibly about young men coming into Ludlow for a fair, but in its talk of 'the lads that will die in their glory and never be old' and who will carry the truth to the grave, it seems to prefigure the violence to come. This does reflect the fact that Housman wrote *A Shropshire Lad* in the shadow of the Second Boer War, but Butterworth's music and, indeed, his death on the Somme in 1916 bring out new resonances to the text.

6   For a revealing account of the Live and Let Live System which emerged in some parts of The Line, see Tony Ashworth, *Trench Warfare, 1914–18: The Live and Let Live System* (London: Pan, 2000). Desultory action was undertaken for the sake of a relatively quiet life. In those sectors, established troops would often fear the arrival of elite units – from either side – whose professionalism or regimental spirit would lead to the battle becoming 'hot'.

7   For a masterful meditation on the generic myths of the war – a Bible or watch saving a life – and the (synechdochal) way his own grandfather represents all grandfathers, see Geoff Dyer, *The Missing of the Somme* (Harmondsworth: Penguin, 1994). This book has exercised a huge influence over my own. At times it has functioned as a *vade mecum* for the path I've sought to follow.

Chapter One

1   It was only later that I began to think it was precisely because it was a tremendous and terrible 'thing', which had directly affected their parents and them, that they might not want to watch.

2   The Churches Together in Britain and Ireland booklet *Beyond Our Tears* (produced in association with the Royal British Legion) now provides for a variety of provision. While this is to the good, I sense that in many churches it will be some time yet before Binyon's words lose their resonance.

3   Geoff Dyer, *The Missing of the Somme* (Harmondsworth: Penguin, 1994), 7.

4   Alan Wilkinson, *The Church of England in the First World War* (London: SPCK, 1978), 294.

5   Dyer, 7.

6   Henri Barbusse, *Under Fire* (London & New York: Dent Dutton, 1965 (1916)), 328.

7   Pindar, Nemean VIII, 40–2, translated by Martha Nussbaum in *The Fragility of Goodness* (Cambridge: Cambridge University Press, 1986), 1.

8   See Rachel Mann, *Dazzling Darkness: Gender, Sexuality, Illness & God* (Glasgow: Wild Goose, 2012). Martha Nussbaum, *The Fragility of Goodness* (Cambridge: Cambridge University Press, 1986).

9   Thomas Carlyle, 'Signs of the Times' (http://www.victorianweb.org/authors/carlyle/signs1.html, 1829).

10 Thomas Carlyle, *Sartor Resartus: The Life and Opinions of Herr Teufelsdröckh; on Heroes, Hero-Worship & the Heroic in History* (London: Everyman, 1908 (1967)), xiv.

11 I sense that this image of eternal rest remains the dominant cultural narrative around death to this day.

12 James E. Young, *The Texture of Memory: Holocaust Memorials and Meaning* (New Haven: Yale University Press, 1994).

13 Ibid., 28.

14 T.S. Eliot, *Selected Poems* (London: Faber, 1954), 53.

15 See W.H.R. Rivers, *Medicine, Magic and Religion* (London: Routledge, 2001). L.A. Hoffman, *Covenant of Blood* (Chicago: University of Chicago, 1996). Melissa L. Meyer, *Thicker Than Water* (London: Routledge, 2005). Mary Douglas, *Purity and Danger* (New York: Praeger, 1966), et al.

Chapter Two

1   In terms of facts about the Church of England during the Great War, this chapter is profoundly indebted to the pioneering historical work of Alan Wilkinson and Albert Marrin.

2   H.H. Henson, 'The Church of England after the War', in F.J. Foakes-Jackson (ed.) *The Faith and the War* (London: Macmillan, 1915), 248

3   Albert Marrin, *The Last Crusade* (Durham NC: Duke University Press, 1974), 177–8.

4   During the first two years of the war, organisations like SPCK distributed over forty million Bibles, hymn books, prayer books and tracts. I do not know if either Grandad Sam or Bert behaved like Davie, one of the old rural folk mentioned in Blythe's *Akenfield*, who had a New Testament 'which he alternately smoked or used for lavatory paper.' Given the often primitive and dreadful circumstances of life in both France and the Middle East, one would be unsurprised if they had.

5   Notably the Christian Socialists.

6   Marrin, 181–2.

7   See Bob Holman, *Woodbine Willie – an Unsung Hero of World War One* (Oxford: Lion, 2013). Studdert Kennedy, who was Vicar of St Paul's, Worcester both before and after the War. One of the intriguing intersections between him and my grandfathers is that 'Willie' – in the early part of the war a chaplain to the training depot of the Worcesters – might well have preached to them at Norton Barracks.

8   Again, Studdert Kennedy was considered a rare exception to this.

9   Alan Wilkinson, *The Church of England in the First World War* (London: SPCK, 1978), 2.

10 Even among the war poets, Owen's work is not, in my view, definitive. David Jones' *In Parenthesis* represents a greater achievement. I shall discuss it later in this book.

11 Wilkinson, 113.

12 Ibid.

13 Harold Owen and John Bell (eds), *Wilfred Owen: Collected Letters* (London: Oxford University Press, 1967), 562.

14 Ibid.

15 Modris Eksteins, *The Rites of Spring* (London: Anchor Doubleday, 1989), 236.

16 Paul Fussell, *The Great War and Modern Memory* (Oxford: Oxford University Press, 1975 (2005)), 26.

17 Wilkinson, 12.

18 Holman, 70.

19 Wilkinson, 188.

20 The Derby Scheme was a project to determine whether British army manpower needs could be met by volunteers alone or whether conscription was necessary. Derby (named after its grand panjandrum, Lord Derby) required every man between 18 and 41, not in a reserved occupation, to declare his availability. When it was announced many men decided to volunteer anyway. It led to 320,000 fit men joining. Nonetheless, 38% of single men and over 54% of married men publicly refused to enlist. This led directly to the introduction of conscription.

21 Marrin, 190.

22 Owen and Bell (eds), 534.

23 Gillian Rose, *Love's Work* (London: Chatto & Windus, 1995).

24 Jon Stallworthy (ed.), *Wilfred Owen: The War Poems* (London: Chatto & Windus, 1994), xix.

25 One is reminded of that quip of Harold Macmillan's about Anthony Eden: 'The trouble with [him] was that he was trained to win the Derby in 1938; unfortunately he was not let out of the starting stalls until 1955.' The Church of England mobilised magnificently in all sorts of way during the Great War, but it was an institution shaped for another world than the one which confronted it.

26 Stallworthy (ed.), 61.

27 See Pat Barker, *Regeneration* (Harmondsworth: Penguin, 1992), 149.

28 Sue Mansfield, *The Rites of War* (London: Bellew, 1991), 131.

29 Paul Tillich makes a potent, still relevant point about fanaticism: '[It] is the correlate to spiritual self-surrender: it shows the anxiety it was supposed to conquer ... the weakness of the fanatic is that those whom he fights have a secret hold upon him; and to this weakness he and his group finally succumb' (*The Courage to Be*, p. 50) cited in Mansfield 1991.

30 Quoted in: Patrick Howarth, *Play Up and Play the Game* (London: Eyre Methuen, 1973), 7.

31 Owen and Bell (eds), 461.

32 Ibid., 590. This letter, dated 29 October 1918, was to prove Owen's penultimate (recorded) letter.

Chapter Three

1   F. Scott Fitzgerald, *Tender Is the Night* (Harmondsworth: Penguin, 1986), 67.
2   On what possible real grounds can the Somme be called a battle? It is, as Paul Fussell suggests, the desire on the part of some military historians to lay the conventions of previous centuries onto what the soldiers more appropriated called the 'Great Fuck-Up'.
3   John Keegan, *The First World War* (London: Hutchinson, 1998), 311.
4   Lord Kitchener is perhaps most famous now for the 'Your Country Needs You!' posters on which his face appeared. The reworking of the poster has become ubiquitous. Indeed, arguably Kitchener has been turned into Kitsch.
5   During the American Civil War there were similar arrangements, in which towns and communities organised battalions and regiments. As a result of the (then) unprecedented slaughter, whole communities lost their men. British recruitment policy had not learned from that. As previously noted the American Civil War – with its experience of trench/siege warfare, the emergence of the machine gun and artillery as defining weapons and the impact of inadequate medicine upon survival rates – offered countless lessons to the combatants of the Great War. Britain – over-confident about its mighty navy as its main element of power and an army made for colonial combat – simply paid inadequate attention to these lessons.
6   To get a sense of perspective, a pre-war British battalion comprised around 1000 men and 35 officers.
7   Keegan, 312.
8   The faith the High Command had in its artillery assault needs to be balanced against an anxiety regarding the reliability of the new Army. One reason that's been offered for the order to move forward in line is a belief at a high level that Kitchener's army wasn't good enough to pull off classic infantry tactics.
9   Paul Fussell, *The Great War and Modern Memory* (Oxford: Oxford University Press, 1975 (2005)), 29.
10 Siegfried Sassoon, *Memoirs of an Infantry Officer* (London: Faber, 2000 (1930)), 71.
11 Max Arthur, *Forgotten Voices of the Great War* (London: Ebury, 2002), 159.
12 There are other ways of telling Nevill's story. Some have suggested that the footballs were pure kidology and bravado – that he and his colleagues knew it was going to be a bloodbath and sought any means to encourage the men. The kicking of footballs into no-man's-land during attacks became something of a 'tradition' for the East Surrey's.
13 Edmund Blunden, *The Mind's Eye: Essays* (London: Jonathan Cape, 1934), 38. See also, Edmund Blunden, *Undertones of War* (London: Collins, 1978 (1928)).
14 Niall Ferguson, *The Pity of War* (London: Allen Lane, 1998), 293.
15 Fussell, 14.
16 The 'Mad Minute' was a term used by the British Army to describe scoring 15 hits onto a 12" round target at 300 yards (270 m) within one minute using a bolt-action rifle. Some Great War soldiers could readily exceed that score. Many riflemen could average 30+ shots while the record, set in 1914

by Sergeant Instructor Alfred Snoxall, was 38 hits. Famously, during the Battle of Mons in August 1914, there were numerous German accounts of coming up against what they believed was machine gun fire when in fact it was squads of riflemen firing at this rate. The intensity of training required to achieve the Mad Minute was not commonly available to the New Army Kitchener Formations.

17 It is unsurprising that those stories have been used for plays like Peter Whelan's 1981 classic *The Accrington Pals* and my own co-written show, *The Tree of War*. (Music and lyrics by Oliver Mills, Book and lyrics by Rachel Mann. Premiered Manchester, September 2015.)

18 Robert Roberts, *The Classic Slum* (Harmondsworth: Penguin, 1986), 80.

19 Ibid., 85.

20 I shall examine this idea more fully in the chapter on 'wounds'. Pat Barker makes much of the impact of 'passivity' and 'submissiveness' on the emotional well-being of 'masculine selves' in her novel *Regeneration*. For a substantial and accessible account of so-called 'shell-shock' see Ben Shephard, *A War of Nerves: Soldiers and Psychiatrists 1914–1994* (London: Pimlico, 2002).

21 Alistair Horne, *The Price of Glory: Verdun 1916* (Harmondsworth: Penguin, 1964), 338.

Chapter Four

1 See Philip Larkin, *The Whitsun Weddings* (London: Faber, 1964).

2 'Variety', trans. Malcolm Cowley, NY 1927, 27-28, quoted in Eksteins, 257.

3 Vera Brittain, *Testament of Youth* (London: Gollancz, 1933).

4 It was hamstrung almost from its inception by Woodrow Wilson's inability to get Senate to ratify it and by the way the designated 'aggressor' nations were excluded. Bolshevik Russia's absence almost ensured it would lack authority. The later withdrawal of Fascist Italy, Nazi Germany and Imperial Japan, among others, essentially finished it off.

5 Modris Eksteins, *The Rites of Spring* (London: Anchor Doubleday, 1989), 256.

6 Eksteins' book represents a dazzling, sustained interrogation of this idea.

7 For more, see Paul Fussell, *The Great War and Modern Memory* (Oxford: Oxford University Press, 1975 (2005)).

8 See Max Arthur, *Forgotten Voices of the Great War* (London: Ebury, 2002).

9 See Ronald Skirth, *The Reluctant Tommy* (London: MacMillan, 2010).

10 The commonly reiterated claim is that the Ottoman Empire was 'the sick man of Europe'. This reflects all sorts of 'orientalist' prejudices. In contrast, there is much evidence to suggest that the Ottomans had something of a modernising renaissance in the late nineteenth and early twentieth centuries.

11 Most notably, *Downton Abbey*, but also *Upstairs, Downstairs* (both in its classic and modern versions) and films like *Gosford Park*.

12 Pre- (and often post-) War these promotions of the humble were almost inconceivable, not least due to the sheer cost of maintaining mess bills and the accoutrements of a commission in peacetime.

13 One of the striking moments in the 1981 film *Chariots of Fire* is the shot, at the start of the film, of the roll of honour in Gonville & Caius College

and the Master's speech about the glorious dead. It becomes clear that the new students are to become the surrogate dead. Indeed, *Chariots of Fire* is – perhaps because of its focus on manly athletic endeavour and identity – as much about the Great War as class or religion. It is soaked in the War: its opening focuses on returning students as the surrogate dead and the end has a scene in which Abrahams arrives back at Waterloo *(the* great war station) with a newspaper headline saying 'Our boys back home'. It both offers readings for and against the war, with Liddell representing the power and impressiveness of conscientious objection; at the same time, it does not mock manly action rewarded in the sporting field (the field of war), in which some fall in the mud (but fall with public school style) and others sacrifice themselves (Lord Lindsay). Abrahams, the Jewish outsider who arrived in France too late to fight, is ambiguous precisely because he doesn't fight in a sporting way and yet he is loved by his comrades because of his courage and passion. He is the definition of foreign and alien – the outsider who breaks up the traditional relations between the classes and England's settled way of going on. Arguably, he represents the War itself.

Chapter Five

1 Charles Loch Mowat, *Britain between the Wars* (London: Methuen, 1987), 6.
2 Nonetheless only those women over thirty were enfranchised and then only if she or her husband were qualified on the local government franchise by owning or occupying land or premises of an annual value of £5.
3 Rosina Harrison, *Rose: My Life in Service* (London: Cassel, 1975), 24.
4 Virginia Nicholson, *Singled Out* (London: Viking, 2007), 78.
5 Ibid.
6 Harrison, 260-61.
7 One of the salutary experiences in my life came when I lived in Jamaica in the early 1990s. I'd arrived full of the easy liberal/radical attitudes of youth. A young woman of the village where I worked presented herself at my door telling me she was, for a small fee, here to do my washing. My response was, 'Don't be absurd, I can do my own washing.' It seemed ridiculous and unjust to me that I – a privileged white person – should have or need someone to 'work for me', to act as a kind of servant, especially when she was a Black Jamaican. I sent her away. This caused a mini scandal in the village. I was seen as denying someone a job – their usual job. No one could understand my scruples (I'm not sure I can myself now). Finally I offered the woman her job back and paid her more. The flabby western liberal in me is ultimately very glad I did. Washing clothes in a river is appalling, back-breaking work. But still, this was that woman's livelihood.
8 The likes of Stalin, Pol Pot and Mao, who *were* prepared to create social catastrophe to enact change surely demonstrate this point.
9 Paul Fussell, *The Great War and Modern Memory* (Oxford: Oxford University Press, 1975 (2005)), 24.
10 Geoff Dyer, *The Missing of the Somme* (Harmondsworth: Penguin, 1994), 6.

11 Raphael Samuel, *Theatres of Memory: Past & Present in Contemporary Culture* (London: Verso, 1994).

12 Dyer, 37.

13 Rachel Mann, *Dazzling Darkness: Gender, Sexuality, Illness & God* (Glasgow: Wild Goose, 2012).

Chapter Six

1 'Words of Institution' refers to the words attributed to Jesus on the night he was betrayed to institute the Eucharist; 'Epiclesis' refers to the invocation of the Holy Spirit during the Eucharistic Prayer.

2 Indeed, the increase in interest in spiritualism during this era was not simply to do with the excess of death and the fact that those who were found were not repatriated, but perhaps the absence of bodies to bury. For what sense of the resurrection of the body might there be in the absence of a body? If loved ones were to be said to have 'persisted through death' in what sense might that be, except in spirit?

3 Modris Eksteins, *The Rites of Spring* (London: Anchor Doubleday, 1989), 107-08.

4 Sue Mansfield, *The Rites of War* (London: Bellew, 1991), 127.

5 Geoff Dyer, *The Missing of the Somme* (Harmondsworth: Penguin, 1994), 13.

6 George L. Mosse, *Fallen Soldiers* (Oxford: Oxford University Press, 1990), 39.

7 Dyer, 14.

8 Bob Bushaway, 'Name Upon Name: The Great War and Remembrance', in *Myths of the English*, ed. by Roy Porter (Cambridge: Polity, 1993), 150.

9 It is worth noting that one of the issues regarding the upkeep of the German graveyards is that, unlike the Commonwealth graves, they are maintained via voluntary subscription.

10 Philip Jenkins, *The Great and Holy War: How World War 1 Changed Religion for Ever* (Oxford: Lion Hudson, 2014), 32.

11 Bushaway, 140.

12 Ibid., 148.

13 Ibid., 139.

14 Ibid., 142.

15 Dyer, 54.

16 Or if the memorials had a purpose it lay in a focus for devotion/worship or in encouraging reflective leisure. So, for example, in Clovelly, Devon, there is a little park dedicated to the fallen. I've already mentioned Gheluvelt Park in Worcester. The memorial spaces united around the concept of 'rest' – a fundamental Christian notion represented by Sunday Worship and Sunday Leisure.

17 The psychological and physical isolation and separation suffered by some soldiers should not be understated. It is clear that the depredations suffered by POWs under Japanese control were sometimes utterly extraordinary.

18 Charles Loch Mowat, *Britain between the Wars* (London: Methuen, 1987), 9.

19 Rachel Mann, *Dazzling Darkness: Gender, Sexuality, Illness & God* (Glasgow: Wild Goose, 2012).

Chapter Seven

1 In Adrien's case he is eventually seen for 'who he is' by the woman, Clemence, with whom he had a fleeting pre-battle romance. In the novel, they ultimately marry.

2 Based on real-life psychiatrist W.H.R Rivers.

3 Ben Shephard, *A War of Nerves: Soldiers and Psychiatrists 1914–1994* (London: Pimlico, 2002), 109. Shephard's superb history of military psychiatry provides detailed factual analysis of the phenomenon of 'shell-shock'. His assiduous work is a key reference point for the facts outlined in this chapter.

4 Ibid., 28.

5 For extensive accounts of the examples previously cited, see ibid., xvii–xviii; ibid.

6 Isabel Colegate, *The Shooting Party* (Harmondsworth: Penguin, 1980).

7 The estimated number of worldwide casualties.

8 It was only late in the war that 'movement' and 'dash' became significant again to its prosecution; by then, the dominant representations of the war had been set

9 Elisabeth Bronfen, *Over Her Dead Body: Death, Femininity, and the Aesthetic* (Manchester: Manchester University Press, 1992).

10 J.L. Carr, *A Month in the Country* (Harmondsworth: Penguin, 1980).

11 Monica Lott, 'Dorothy L. Sayers, the Great War and Shell Shock', *Interdisciplinary Literary Studies*, 15 (2013), 104.

12 Ibid.

13 Ibid.

14 It should be noted that either consciously or unconsciously Sayers deploys a version of a well-established nineteenth-century literary trope: the wounded man as the only man fit for marriage to a strong, assertive woman. Charlotte Brontë's *Jane Eyre* is perhaps the acme of the trope. However, equally significant is Elizabeth Barrett Browning's novel-poem *Aurora Leigh*. Indeed, its picture (admittedly, somewhat more grandiose than Sayers') of Aurora and blind Romney's marriage as a new birth of heaven on earth offers a striking precursor of Peter and Harriet's union. Clearly, many would argue that 'marriage' by its very nature is a conservative, patriarchal institution. However, as I and others have argued, under conditions of patriarchy, a marriage (like that in *Aurora Leigh* and *Busman's Honeymoon*) constructed around equality can actually be feminist and liberative.

Chapter Eight

1 This memorial commemorates events that happened in this sector of the war unconnected to 1 July 1916.

2 Sebastian Faulks, *Birdsong* (London: Hutchinson, 1993 (2004)).

3 Geoffrey Hill, *Selected Poems* (London: Penguin, 2006), 34.

4 See Shakespeare's *Henry V* for a famous literary representation of this fact. Post-battle, the herald reports the English dead thus: 'Edward the Duke of

York, the Earl of Suffolk,/Sir Richard Ketly, Davy Gam, esquire:/None else of name.'

5   David Jones, *In Parenthesis* (London: Faber, 1937 (1990)).
6   Paul Fussell, *The Great War and Modern Memory* (Oxford: Oxford University Press, 1975 (2005)), 146.
7   Ibid., 146.
8   Ibid., 154.
9   Jay Winter, *Sites of Memory, Sites of Mourning* (Cambridge: Canto, 1995), 5.

Chapter Nine

1   I've explored ideas in this chapter in: Rachel Mann, 'Nostalgia and the New: The Unavoidability of the Great War' (Torquay: The Hinksey Network, 2005).
2   Barbara Brown Taylor, *When God Is Silent* (Cambridge MA.: Cowley, 1998), 9.
3   Ibid., 19.
4   Ibid., 23.
5   Ibid.
6   Ibid.
7   Geoff Dyer, *The Missing of the Somme* (Harmondsworth: Penguin, 1994),, 27.
8   Ibid., 28.
9   Elaine Scarry, *The Body in Pain* (Oxford: Oxford University Press, 1985), 63.
10 Ibid., 64. Scarry indicates that only that military writer manqué, Von Clausewitz, is honest and clear-eyed about the nature and purposes of war.
11 The Freudian connotations of this, added to by the notion of Scarry's idea of injuring as a 'deflationary' move, are almost too vulgar to enumerate.
12 Paul Fussell, *The Great War and Modern Memory* (Oxford: Oxford University Press, 1975 (2005)), 21. Fussell's thinking in this area has been an incalculable aid to my own. My thoughts are, at best, footnotes on his.
13 Ibid., 24.
14 Ibid.
15 Ibid., 288.
16 E.R. Dodds, *The Greeks and the Irrational* (Berkeley: University of California, 1951), 102.
17 J. Jeremy Wisnewski and R.D. Emerick, *The Ethics of Torture* (London: Continuum, 2009).
18 Jay Winter, *Sites of Memory, Sites of Mourning* (Cambridge: Canto, 1995).
19 Stanley Cavell, *Must We Mean What We Say?: A Book of Essays* (New York: Scribner, 1969), 302.

Postscript

1   David Stevenson, *1914–1918* (London: Penguin, 2004), 569.
2   Modris Eksteins, *The Rites of Spring* (London: Anchor Doubleday, 1989), 258.
3   Stevenson, xix.
4   For example, it concentrates almost entirely on the military prosecution of the war and the myths about Haig's personality in particular; it lacks any

appreciation of the political or economic nuances of the conflict. Although, I suspect, concentrating on those would hardly rank as entertainment.

5   Timothy Findlay, *The Wars* (Toronto: Penguin, 1977 (1978)), 71–2.

Select Bibliography

Max Arthur, *Forgotten Voices of the Great War* (London: Ebury, 2002)
Tony Ashworth, *Trench Warfare, 1914–18: The Live and Let Live System* (London: Pan, 2000)

Henri Barbusse, *Under Fire* (London & New York: Dent Dutton, 1965 (1916))
Pat Barker, *Regeneration* (Harmondsworth: Penguin, 1992)
Edmund Blunden, *The Mind's Eye: Essays* (London: Jonathan Cape, 1934)
———, *Undertones of War* (London: Collins, 1978 (1928))
Vera Brittain, *Testament of Youth* (London: Gollancz, 1933)
Elisabeth Bronfen, *Over Her Dead Body: Death, Femininity, and the Aesthetic* (Manchester: Manchester University Press, 1992)
Barbara Brown Taylor, *When God Is Silent* (Cambridge MA.: Cowley, 1998)
Bob Bushaway, 'Name Upon Name: The Great War and Remembrance', in *Myths of the English*, ed. by Roy Porter (Cambridge: Polity, 1993)

Thomas Carlyle, *Sartor Resartus: The Life and Opinions of Herr Teufelsdröckh; on Heroes, Hero-Worship & the Heroic in History* (London: Everyman, 1908 (1967))
———, 'Signs of the Times' (1829) [Accessed 20/12 2015]
J.L. Carr, *A Month in the Country* (Harmondsworth: Penguin, 1980)
Stanley Cavell, *Must We Mean What We Say?: A Book of Essays* (New York: Scribner, 1969)
Isabel Colegate, *The Shooting Party* (Harmondsworth: Penguin, 1980)

E.R. Dodds, *The Greeks and the Irrational* (Berkeley University of California, 1951)
Mary Douglas, *Purity and Danger* (New York: Praeger, 1966)
Geoff Dyer, *The Missing of the Somme* (Harmondsworth: Penguin, 1994)

Modris Eksteins, *The Rites of Spring* (London: Anchor Doubleday, 1989)
T.S. Eliot, *Selected Poems* (London: Faber, 1954)

Sebastian Faulks, *Birdsong* (London: Hutchinson 1993 (2004))
Niall Ferguson, *The Pity of War* (London: Allen Lane, 1998)

Timothy Findlay, *The Wars* (Toronto: Penguin, 1977 (1978))
Paul Fussell, *The Great War and Modern Memory* (Oxford: Oxford University Press, 1975 (2005))

Rosina Harrison, *Rose: My Life in Service* (London: Cassel, 1975)
H.H. Henson, 'The Church of England after the War', in F.J. Foakes-Jackson (ed.) *The Faith and the War* (London: Macmillan, 1915)
Geoffrey Hill, *Selected Poems* (London: Penguin, 2006)
L.A. Hoffman, *Covenant of Blood* (Chicago: University of Chicago, 1996)
Bob Holman, *Woodbine Willie – an Unsung Hero of World War One* (Oxford: Lion, 2013)
Richard Holmes, *War Walks: From Agincourt to Normandy* (London: BBC, 1996)
Alistair Horne, *The Price of Glory: Verdun 1916* (Harmondsworth: Penguin, 1964)
Patrick Howarth, *Play Up and Play the Game* (London: Eyre Methuen, 1973)

Philip Jenkins, *The Great and Holy War: How World War 1 Changed Religion for Ever* (Oxford: Lion Hudson, 2014)
David Jones, *In Parenthesis* (London: Faber, 1937 (1990))

John Keegan, *The First World War* (London: Hutchinson, 1998)

Philip Larkin, *The Whitsun Weddings* (London: Faber, 1964)
Charles Loch Mowat, *Britain between the Wars* (London: Methuen, 1987)
Monica Lott, 'Dorothy L. Sayers, the Great War and Shell Shock', *Interdisciplinary Literary Studies*, 15 (2013)

Rachel Mann, *Dazzling Darkness: Gender, Sexuality, Illness & God* (Glasgow: Wild Goose, 2012)
———, 'Nostalgia and the New: The Unavoidability of the Great War' (Torquay: The Hinksey Network, 2005)
Sue Mansfield, *The Rites of War* (London: Bellew, 1991)
Albert Marrin, *The Last Crusade* (Durham NC: Duke University Press, 1974)
Melissa L. Meyer, *Thicker Than Water* (London: Routledge, 2005)
George L. Mosse, *Fallen Soldiers* (Oxford: Oxford University Press, 1990)

Virginia Nicholson, *Singled Out* (London: Viking, 2007)
Martha Nussbaum, *The Fragility of Goodness* (Cambridge: Cambridge University Press, 1986)

Harold Owen, and John Bell (eds) *Wilfred Owen: Collected Letters* (London: Oxford University Press, 1967)

Select Bibliography

W.H.R. Rivers, *Medicine, Magic and Religion* (London: Routledge, 2001)
Robert Roberts, *The Classic Slum* (Harmondsworth: Penguin, 1986)
Gillian Rose, *Love's Work* (London: Chatto & Windus, 1995)

Raphael Samuel, *Theatres of Memory: Past & Present in Contemporary Culture* (London: Verso, 1994)
Siegfried Sassoon, *Memoirs of an Infantry Officer* (London: Faber, 2000 (1930))
Elaine Scarry, *The Body in Pain* (Oxford: Oxford University Press, 1985)
F. Scott Fitzgerald, *Tender Is the Night* (Harmondsworth: Penguin, 1986)
Ben Shephard, *A War of Nerves: Soldiers and Psychiatrists 1914–1994* (London: Pimlico, 2002)
Ronald Skirth, *The Reluctant Tommy* (London: Macmillan, 2010)
Jon Stallworthy (ed). *Wilfred Owen: The War Poems* (London: Chatto & Windus, 1994)
David Stevenson, *1914–1918* (London: Penguin, 2004)

Alan Wilkinson, *The Church of England in the First World War* (London: SPCK, 1978)
Jay Winter, *Sites of Memory, Sites of Mourning* (Cambridge: Canto, 1995)
J. Jeremy Wisnewski, and R.D. Emerick, *The Ethics of Torture* (London: Continuum, 2009)

James E. Young, *The Texture of Memory: Holocaust Memorials and Meaning* (New Haven: Yale University Press, 1994)